NEAB

GCSE English

Imelda Pilgrim

Principal Examiner for NEAB English

Consultants: Peter Buckroyd
Chief Examiner for NEAB English

John Nield
Principal Examiner for NEAB English

Heinemann Educational Publishers
Halley Court, Jordan Hill, Oxford OX2 8EJ

OXFORD   MADRID   ATHENS   FLORENCE
PRAGUE   CHICAGO   PORTSMOUTH NH (USA)
MEXICO CITY   SÃO PAULO   SINGAPORE
KUALA LUMPUR   TOKYO   MELBOURNE
AUCKLAND   NAIROBI   KAMPALA
IBADAN   GABORONE   JOHANNESBURG

First published 1997

2001 2000 99 98 97
10 9 8 7 6 5 4

ISBN 0 435 10132 3

Designed and produced by Gecko Ltd, Bicester, Oxon
Cover illustration by MCC
Illustrations by Phillip Bannister, pp125, 126; Lee Ebrell, pp123, 124; Max Ellis, pp105, 135; Phylis Mahon, p133; David Mitcheson, pp108, 142–143, 153; Pantelis Palios, pp12, 104, 118, 120; Gary Wing, pp116, 127, 134.
Printed and bound in Spain by Mateu Cromo

Acknowledgements
The Authors and Publishers should like to thank the following for permission to use copyright material.
Mail on Sunday/Solo Syndication for the newspaper editorial, p14; *The Guardian* for the letter by Sian Prescott, p15; the advertisement for VO5 Select shampoo from *Zest* magazine, October 1996, p16 was reproduced courtesy of Alberto-Culver UK Ltd and National Magazines; the advertisement for Vosene Frequent, p17 was reproduced with kind permission from Vosene; John Brown Publishing Ltd for the front cover of *Fortean Times* on p18; EMAP Pursuit Ltd for the front cover of *Sported!* magazine, p18; *Daily Mail*/Solo Syndication for the newspaper headline, p18; Express Newspapers plc for the newspaper headline, p19; the Amnesty International leaflet headline, p19 was reproduced courtesy of Amnesty International UK, 99–119 Rosebery Ave, London EC1R 4RE; letter from Shelter reproduced by kind permission of Shelter, the National Campaign for Homeless People, p20; Consumers' Association for extracts from *Which?* March 1996, *Which?* June 1996, *Which?* January 1997 published by Consumers' Association, 2 Marylebone Road, London NW1 4DF. To find out more, including how to get *Which?* free for 3 months, please write to Department A3, FREEPOST, Hertford SG14 1YB or telephone free on 0800 252100, pp21–22; Express Newspapers plc for the article on pp24–25; Gordon Styles, Teesside Business Executive of the Year 1996, Managing Director of Styles Precision Components Ltd and *Inform* magazine for the article, p29; Express Newspapers plc for the article on p30; the Bowes Museum, Barnard Castle, Co Durham for 'Fashions in Jane Austen's Time', p32; the extract on p33 is from *Timelines: Clothes*, first published in the UK by Franklin Watts, a division of the Watts Publishing Group, 96 Leonard St, London EC2A 4RH; *The Independent* for the problem page, p34; HarperCollins Publishers Ltd for the definition from the *Collins English Dictionary*, p35; Faber and Faber Ltd for the extract from *Writing Home* by Alan Bennett, p35; Edinburgh and Lothians Tourist Board for 'So Much to See and Do' from *The Essential Guide to Edinburgh*, p42; the extracts on pp43 and 50–1 are © Bill Bryson 1995. Extracted from *Notes from a Small Island* published by Black Swan, a division of Transworld Publishers Ltd. All rights reserved; 'Bedale – Gateway to the Dales' is from the Hambleton Visitor Guide, *Come and Stay in Herriot Country*, produced by Hambleton District Council, p49; *Sugar* magazine, Issue no 21, July 1996 for 'Hot Summer Cuts', p58; EMAP Pursuit Ltd for the extract from *Sported!* magazine, p58; *Fortean Times*/John Brown Publishing Ltd for the extract on p60; 'To Newcastle-upon-Tyne' from *An English Journey* by Beryl Bainbridge by permission of Gerald Duckworth & Co Ltd, p60; Great Ormond Street Hospital Children's Charity for the fundraising advertisement, p61; the Health Education Authority for 'Throwing light on sunrays', reproduced with permission, p63; Butlin's for the brochure extract, p65; the brochure extract on p67 was reproduced by kind permission of Club 18–30; Scholastic Children's Books for the extract from *Horrible Histories – Cruel Kings and Mean Queens* by Terry Deary 1995, p69; *Northallerton, Thirsk and Bedale Times* for the news report, p72; *The Guardian* for the news report, p72; ACTIONAID for the extract on p73; *Woman and Home* for the article on p75; Dan Williams for the two cartoons, p75; the article on p76 was reproduced by permission of Roger St Pierre, Editor, *Cycling and Mountain Biking Today*; *The Journal* for the letter by E. D. Irving, p79; the Department of Transport for 'What would you kill for?', pp81–83; the Health Education Authority for 'Your Children & Drugs – Magic Mushrooms', p84; 'It's easy to be green' extract reproduced by kind permission of Halifax plc and taken from the Halifax *Quest* magazine, written by Tim Gill, TEXT Professional Writing Services, p92; *Daily Mail*/Solo Syndication for the article by David Norris, p93; the cartoon, p93 is © K Meehan. First published in *Essential Articles 4*, the resource file for issues, Carel Press; the World Wide Fund For Nature for 'Rhinoceros', pp96–7; the Estate of Vivienne de Watteville for 'Taking a Picture' from *Speak to the Earth* by Vivienne de Watteville, published by Methuen, pp98–9; the Author for 'Nettles' and 'Uncle Edward's Affliction' by Vernon Scannell, pp105–6; Faber and Faber Ltd for 'Tich Miller' from *Making Cocoa for Kingsley Amis* by Wendy Cope, p108; 'Toads' by Philip Larkin is reprinted from *The Less Deceived* by permission of The Marvell Press, England and Australia, p112; Faber and Faber Ltd for 'Toads Revisited' from *The Whitsun Weddings* by Philip Larkin, p113; 'November Night' from *Verse* by Adelaide Crapsey. Copyright 1922 by Algernon S Crapsey and renewed 1950 by The Adelaide Crapsey Foundation. Reprinted by permission of Alfred A Knopf Inc, p115; 'Fog' from *Chicago Poems* by Carl Sandburg, copyright 1916 by Holt, Rinehart and Winston, Inc. and renewed 1944 by Harcourt Brace & Company, reprinted by permission of Harcourt Brace & Company, p116; Faber and Faber Ltd for the extract from 'The Love Song of J. Alfred Prufrock' from *Collected Poems 1909–1962* by T. S. Eliot, p116; Michael Horovitz for 'Sea's cape' from *Growing Up: Selected Poems and Pictures 1951–79*, published by Allison & Busby, 1979, p119; Edinburgh University Press for 'Inventory' from *Dreaming Frankenstein* by Liz Lochhead, published by Polygon in 1984, p120; 'Nooligan' by Roger McGough from *I See A Voice*. Reprinted by permission of The Peters Fraser and Dunlop Group Limited on behalf of © Roger McGough, p121; 'The Identification' by Roger McGough from *Strictly Private*. Reprinted by permission of The Peters Fraser and Dunlop Group Limited on behalf of © Roger McGough, p123; Tony Harrison for 'Long Distance', p124; 'Poem' from *Zoom!* by Simon Armitage (Bloodaxe Books, 1989), p125; David Higham Associates for 'Do Not Go Gentle into That Good Night' by Dylan Thomas from *The Poems*, published by J. M. Dent, p126; James MacGibbon for 'Not Waving But Drowning' from *The Collected Poems of Stevie Smith* (Penguin 20th Century Classics), p127; 'Island Man' by Grace Nichols, p132 and three lines on the cover are from *The Fat Black Woman's Poems*, Virago Press, 1984; David Higham Associates for 'Trumpet Player' from *The Collected Poems of Langston Hughes*, published by Vintage US, pp135–6; Virago Press for the extract from *I Know Why the Caged Bird Sings* by Maya Angelou, pp142–3; the article by Matthew Bridgeman, pp147–9, is taken from *Sport* edited by John Foster, by permission of Oxford University Press; Jonathan Cape Ltd for the extract from *Going Solo* by Roald Dahl, p151; the extract from *Of Mice and Men* by John Steinbeck, published by William Heinemann, p152; Hamish Hamilton Ltd for the extract from 'Mr Proudham and Mr Sleight', from *A Bit of Singing and Dancing* by Susan Hill, p154, copyright Susan Hill, 1971, 1972, 1973. All rights reserved.

The Publishers have made every effort to trace the copyright holders, but if they have inadvertently overlooked any, they will be pleased to make the necessary arrangements at the first opportunity.

The Publishers should like to thank the following for permission to reproduce photographs on the pages noted.
British Film Institute, p24; Rex Features, p25; John Walmsley, p80; Imperial War Museum, p107; Oxford Scientific Films, pp112–14; Format, p131; Action-Plus, p148; Camera Press, p155.

Introduction

This book is designed to help you do as well as you possibly can in your NEAB GCSE English examination. Many students ask *how* they can prepare for GCSE English. Other subjects have content to revise so that you can be clear about exactly what you need to know. GCSE English assesses reading and writing skills that you have been developing for almost all of your life. So how can you improve these skills before your examination?

The good news is that because GCSE English concentrates on reading and writing you are already well equipped with the skills you need to succeed. Even better news is that there *are* specific things you can do to make sure you are fully prepared for your examination. You can find out and really understand exactly what each paper will test, then you can make sure you have practised reading the sorts of texts you will find on the exam papers, and practised the writing skills you need as well.

NEAB English ensures you cover exactly what is needed for each examination paper:

Paper 1
- reading and response to non-fiction
- writing to argue, persuade or instruct

Paper 2
- reading and response to poets from the English literary heritage and to poems from other cultures and traditions
- writing to inform, explain or describe.

*A Note About your NEAB Anthology: This book develops the skills you need to respond to the poems in your **NEAB Anthology** and to write about the poems in your examination. It shows you the styles of questions you will meet in the examination and how to answer them. It does not include the specific poems from your **Anthology** because NEAB will alter some of the poems every two years. You will find revision activities for specific poems in **Working with the English Anthology**, from Heinemann.*

About the author
Imelda Pilgrim is an NEAB Principal Examiner for GCSE English and a practising English teacher.

Contents

PAPER 1

Section A: Reading Response to Non-Fiction Texts   **11**

Section B: Writing to Argue, Persuade or Instruct   **57**

PAPER 2

How to use this book

The book takes you through each element of your GCSE English examinations. You will probably find it easiest to work through the sections in the order they appear, although this is not essential.

As you progress through the book you will:

- learn more about the specific skills that you will be tested on in the different papers

- find a wide range of texts and activities designed to help you improve these skills

- work through examples of the kind of questions that are set in the examinations

- receive guidance on how to read the questions carefully

- learn how to plan and develop your answers.

There are also specimen examination papers for you to try, once you have worked through the appropriate sections. Your teacher will tell you whether you should attempt the Foundation or Higher Tier papers.

By reading the suggestions, studying the texts and working through the activities, you will gain not only in awareness of what you are expected to do but also in confidence and competence. The effort you make now will stand you in a good position to face the challenge of the GCSE examinations and will help you to achieve your full potential.

Your skills in English

Although you probably aren't aware of it, you have spent nearly all your life developing your skills in English, from your infant days when you started to use language in speech and to put words together, through those early experiences in reading and writing where you struggled to make sense of simple words in a child's text and to write those same words in a clear form. As a young child your skills in English developed rapidly. Before long you were soon reading whole texts and writing poems, short stories, diaries and letters of your own.

As you progressed through primary and then secondary school you probably ranged more widely in your choice of reading, becoming gradually more aware of the subtleties and complexities of a written text. In writing, you almost certainly started to use a wider and more sophisticated range of vocabulary and sentence structures, becoming ever more conscious of the need to be effective in your personal writing. Now you are in the process of preparing for your GCSE examinations in English. You need to consolidate the skills that you have already acquired, develop some new ones and learn how to use these to your best advantage.

English, in the written examination situation, is about reading and writing. Although these are assessed separately in the examinations, they are very closely linked and often overlap. You will find, therefore, that the work you do on reading has direct implications for your writing and vice versa.

Developing your reading skills

In addition to working through this book, one of the best ways you can help yourself is by doing as much reading as you can. The GCSE years are busy ones and it is easy to neglect private reading when you have so much school work to do. The fact remains, however, that it is through reading a range of materials that you develop an understanding of how they are organized, of how language is being used and of the different ways in which you, the reader, can be affected. Furthermore, you learn new vocabulary, new sentence structures and new ways of organizing ideas, all of which helps you in your own writing. Aim for variety and set some time to one side every day purely for reading for interest and pleasure.

Take more notice of the reading materials around you in your daily life. Start to read leaflets, newsletters, magazine and newspaper articles and adverts with a more critical eye. Think about the way they are written and whether they fit in with what you are learning about presentation and content. Do they successfully target audience and purpose? Above all, are they effective and what makes them so? The more attention and thought you give to the reading materials that surround you, the more you will come to understand how you are influenced by them.

Start today and, as you increase your understanding of how other writers achieve success, you will soon see improvements in your own writing.

Developing your writing skills

Every piece of writing you do, whether it be a diary entry, a letter, notes on a particular topic or an imaginative story, has a specific audience and purpose – you are writing for someone, be it yourself or another person, and you have a reason for doing so. When you are in the process of writing something it is very important that you keep both your audience and purpose in mind so that what you say is both relevant and appropriate.

Different kinds of writing will require different levels of formality – a diary entry is likely to be fairly informal and may be written in non-standard English whilst a letter of application for Work Experience is almost certainly going to be formal and written in standard English. Similarly, different kinds of writing require different levels of planning. It is unlikely that you would carefully plan in advance what you were going to write on a postcard but very likely that you would give a lot of thought and effort to the planning stages of writing a story.

Whatever you are writing you should be constantly thinking of what you want to say and trying to work out the best and most effective way to put it into words. When making notes, for example, you need to be very selective in picking out the key features only and expressing them as concisely as possible. In contrast, when writing a story it is likely that you will be trying to build up the descriptive detail so that your reader can understand and share your ideas and your experience.

Developing greater awareness of how you and other people write is an important element of improving your writing skills. Think about the way sentences are constructed. Look at the way you, and other writers, use words to create a particular effect and start to expand your range of words. Whenever you come across a word you don't understand find out its meaning and try to use it in your own writing. Above all, don't be afraid to experiment with new ideas and new methods. By doing so you will find not only that the quality of your writing improves but that the experience of writing becomes altogether more challenging, exciting and rewarding.

PAPER 1

*This paper examines **Reading** in Section A and **Writing** in Section B. Each section is worth 15% of your final mark for English.*

Section A requires a reading response to unseen non-fiction materials (e.g. one or more extracts from autobiographies, biographies, journals, diaries, letters, travel writing, leaflets, newspaper articles, factual and informative materials).

Section B requires one piece of writing which argues, persuades or instructs, linked to the theme(s) or topic(s) of the stimulus materials in Section A.

Section A:
Reading Response to Non-Fiction Texts

The qualities or skills the examiner will be looking for in your response are known as the Assessment Objectives. These Assessment Objectives form the basis of the NEAB Mark Scheme and are based on your ability to:

- distinguish between fact and opinion
- evaluate how information is presented and show awareness of structural and presentational devices
- follow an argument
- identify implications and recognize inconsistencies
- select material appropriate to purpose
- collate material from different sources.

How this section helps

The following pages take you through these Assessment Objectives, explaining what skills you need and providing examples and activities to help you develop them.

Fact and opinion

> Chocolate is bad for you, and that's a fact!

But is it? If you are overweight or have a physical problem then chocolate probably is bad for you! If, however, you are a mountaineer about to spend the night on a rockface you would almost certainly discover that chocolate is good for you! The statement 'chocolate is bad for you' is really an *opinion*.

How then can we know what is fact and opinion?

ACTIVITY 1

Which of the following statements are **facts** and which are **opinions**?

- In July 1969 the American astronaut, Neil Armstrong, became the first person to walk on the moon.

- The gravitational attraction of the moon causes tides to rise and fall in the earth's oceans.

- Man's landing on the moon is the greatest achievement of the twentieth century.

- The position of the moon directly affects your star sign and the things that are happening in your life.

How did you decide which statements were fact and which were opinion?
How could you check whether you are right?
Did you notice that opinions can be written as though they are facts?

Put simply, a *fact* is something that can be proved to be true whereas an *opinion* cannot. Sometimes, it is not too difficult to tell the difference between fact and opinion. At other times you have to read very carefully to distinguish one from the other.

Check the facts: surveys

Something may be a 'fact' but may be based on very little evidence, or evidence that is misleading. For example:

1 **A survey of cat owners may show that 90% of them use a particular brand of cat food.**

What difference would it make to this 'fact' if the survey was undertaken right next to the supermarket shelves selling that particular brand?

2 **A survey of home owners may show that 74% of them are happy with the nursery provision for children in their area.**

To what extent do the results of this survey depend on the area where it was carried out?

ACTIVITY 2

In a survey carried out by one of the country's leading family experts nearly half of the teenage girls interviewed said that their school had an anti-bullying policy but only four in ten of these believed it actually worked.

Make a list of the questions you would want to ask about this survey before accepting its findings.

Identify opinions

Not all surveys are as unreliable. The survey which annually follows the publication of GCSE results may show that 44.5% of pupils gained a grade C or above in five of their GCSE exams. This is clearly a more reliable fact as the figures take into account all the candidates sitting GCSE exams in a particular year. Even so, this information may then be presented in different ways and the reader has to take care not to be misled. One newspaper might choose to interpret the results in a favourable light, loudly proclaiming:

Another newspaper may use the same statistics for a very different purpose. Imagine the headline:

Our children are getting cleverer and the facts prove it

Recent figures show that more children than ever are achieving grade C in their GCSE exams.

EXAMS GET EASIER AS MORE CHILDREN ACHIEVE GRADE C OR ABOVE

- What fact is used in both headlines?
- What are the different opinions being expressed?
- What impressions do these opinions create?

Neither of these newspapers could prove their claims, yet the opinions they express are based on the same factual evidence.

ACTIVITY 3

Now write your own contradictory headlines for the following survey results.

- Six out of ten teenagers believe it's important to work hard at school.
- Over two-thirds of all teenagers think they will get married but only half of these believe marriage should be for ever.

13

More about opinions: editorials

Most newspapers carry an editorial comment or leader linked to an item that is currently in the news. This is generally an expression of opinion by the editor, designed to influence the way the reader thinks.

The following editorial appeared in a national newspaper on the same day it printed the news that the lottery operator Camelot had 'signed a £15 million deal with an undischarged bankrupt who had links with a Mafia godfather'.

Camelot bosses must hand over their prize

THE National Lottery has been a great success, bringing fun and wealth to lucky winners and thousands of good causes.

Yet, at the same time, there has always been an uneasy feeling about the Lottery operator, Camelot.

Much of this can be put down to sour grapes or the grumblings of killjoys, but today's exclusive revelations that Camelot is doing business with an undischarged bankrupt with an unsavoury past falls into an entirely different category. It lends weight to the suspicion that the owners of Camelot are only interested in making money – and are not too fussy about how, or with whom, they do it.

Ideally, the Lottery Regulator ought to intervene, but unfortunately he has always seemed out of his depth and incapable of effective action.

Whichever party now wins the coming election, it is surely time to review Camelot's monopoly grip on the National Lottery. Why should the state permit one company, and its directors, to become winners while preventing others from offering different, perhaps even better, services?

Whatever happened to competition?

THE MAIL ON SUNDAY

ACTIVITY 4

What is the editor's view about the Lottery operator Camelot?
How does he try to persuade his readers to share this viewpoint?
You should think about:

- the way opinions are stated as facts

- the use of paragraphing for emphasis

- the use of rhetorical questions.

More about opinions: letters

Readers are also given the opportunity to express their views on current issues in the letters pages of magazines and newspapers. These letters mainly express personal opinions. Here is a letter written by a teenage girl in response to a newspaper article in which a parent objected to his daughters being made to play rugby at school.

I AM desperate to play rugby, but denied the chance. I started to play when I was 11 in a mixed team, organized out of school. Unfortunately, I am now too old to play with younger boys and girls, and my school has flatly refused to let me, or any other girls, play rugby.

So I think that those two Gregory girls who refused to participate in rugby training should realize how lucky they are to have the chance to play. There is a big difference between the games and training: the chances of getting hurt are much lower. Providing they wear gumshields, they won't lose teeth.

Now people will think girls as a whole don't want to play rugby when there are millions who haven't been given the chance, and gone to different sports, which is devastating to the game on the international scene.

Rugby has got me fit and I have loved every minute of both training and playing. I used to be very shy. Rugby has made me incredibly confident on and off the field. If girls aren't taken seriously on the rugby field, then they won't be taken seriously anywhere else.

Sian Prescott

The Guardian

ACTIVITY 5

Summarize, in a few sentences, the opinion expressed in the letter. What 'evidence' does the writer use to support her opinion?

Practice

Read both the advertisement below and the one on the opposite page, then complete Activity 6.

Changing your hair colour should be easy. But, by the time you've read through the confusing instructions for most home hair colourants, you're often left with just two choices – chance it and risk disappointment or forget it and carry on dreaming about that ideal colour.

You need dream no more. Hair colour experts Alberto VO5 have made hair colouring easy with new VO5 Select. Its unique VO5 Select Indicator makes it so easy to choose a colour. On one side of the pack you'll find the shade close to your natural colour and on the other, a guide to the expected colour result – it's that simple.

The new VO5 Select range comprises 12 fantastic wash-in, wash-out colours, which last up to eight washes and contain no ammonia or peroxide. It is the first semi-permanent range to include vibrant fashion shades as well as natural shades to cover grey, and the first to be awarded the Plain English Campaign's coveted Crystal Mark for its clear instructions. Each box, costing just £2.99, contains a sealing rinse to condition, protect and reduce colour fading – so your hair will always look its shiny best.

What about application? VO5 Selects' specially designed cap reduces any messy drips, and speeds up the colour development time using the heat from your head. Such a simple approach and a unique money-back guarantee means it's the ideal choice for first-time colourers. In fact, it's perfect for anyone who wants beautifully coloured hair with no fuss!

ACTIVITY 6

1 Copy out and complete this table, entering the details that are clearly fact and opinion and those about which you are not sure.

	FACT	OPINION	NOT SURE
VO5			
VOSENE			

2 Words can be used to influence the reader and to help disguise an opinion.

a Look at the VO5 advertisement:
- List the words and phrases that suggest the product is easy to use.
- What is the effect of the following words?

  dream   fantastic   vibrant   shiny

- What is implied by the following phrases?

  costing just £2.99

  unique money-back guarantee

  the ideal choice

Vosene

FREQUENT

Life's stressful enough without hair hassle, so if you want healthy-looking hair, then try no nonsense Vosene Frequent. The active ingredients leave your hair and scalp really clean.

If you've had a tough day, Vosene Frequent's invigorating fragrance not only leaves your hair smelling fresh but is totally reviving too and helps to shake off everyday stress. It contains special conditioning ingredients too, so you can wash your hair every day and it still stays looking shiny and manageable. And as it's priced at £1.39 for a 200ml bottle and £1.99 for a 300ml bottle, it's not going to put a strain on your wallet either.

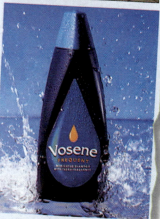

Vosene Frequent is available from all good chemists and supermarkets.

b **Now look at the Vosene advertisement above:**

- How does the wording suggest that the product relieves stress?
- What is the effect of the following words?

  healthy-looking invigorating reviving shiny

- What is implied by the following phrases?

  not going to put a strain on your wallet

  available from all good chemists

3 Try rewriting *one* of these advertisements using factual detail only.

POINTS *to remember*

- A fact is something that can be proved to be true whereas an opinion cannot.
- The results of a survey may be misleading.
- Opinion can be mixed with fact and you need to separate the two.
- Opinion is sometimes presented as though it were fact.

How information is presented

Nowadays we are bombarded with information. Just look at the mail that comes through your letterbox each day. There will be adverts, letters from charities, leaflets and political pamphlets, to name but a few. Go to your doctor or your dentist and you will find news-sheets, leaflets and posters encouraging you to think about different aspects of your health and diet. Walk into any newsagent's and, as well as all the local and national newspapers, you will find a vast number of magazines catering for all age and interest groups.

With so much visual material surrounding you in your daily life, it is essential that you understand its meaning and evaluate the effect it has on you as a reader. You need to be aware of the presentational and structural devices that are being used and the impact that they can have.

Here are some of the most commonly used devices:

Headlines

These are designed to capture the reader's interest. They may be dramatic:

I thought we would never get out alive

THE DAILY MAIL

They may rely heavily on a play on words:

I led dog's life says fired kennel maid

THE DAILY EXPRESS

They may involve the reader by asking a question:

Would you be put in prison if you complained about your school?

AMNESTY INTERNATIONAL

Sub-headings

These are used to separate the text into smaller, more easily managed units and to summarize the content or draw the reader's attention to the main points of interest:

HOW TO LOSE WEIGHT

Follow our tips to a long-term solution – it can be done

By following any diet – no matter how weird or wonderful – most people will lose weight in the short-term. The difficult part is to keep the weight off and not get caught in a cycle of on–off dieting.

Don't watch the clock

First, set yourself a target weight. If you've got a lot of weight to lose, set interim targets, to keep your spirits up. Be realistic about how quickly you can lose weight. You're likely to lose weight faster at the outset, but a weight loss of just 1lb to 2lb a week is recommended as the maximum for most people. Rapid weight loss is bad for you.

Plan your diet

Eat foods that are rich in nutrients – so plenty of fruit and vegetables, and starch foods like pasta and potatoes. Cut down on foods that are high in energy with few nutrients, such as fried snack foods. But don't try to cut out your favourite foods altogether. Strict rules can trigger failure.

Keep active

It's also important to be active. But that doesn't mean you have to join a gym or take up jogging – any type of exercise is beneficial. Just walk instead of getting the bus, for instance.

ACTIVITY 1

How do the headings and sub-headings help to draw you into the article above?

19

Bold print, *italics* and <u>underlining</u>

Any or all of these may be used to draw the reader's attention to a particular point that the writer wishes to emphasize, as is shown in these extracts from a letter written on behalf of the charity Shelter:

Shelter
THE NATIONAL CAMPAIGN FOR HOMELESS PEOPLE
88 Old Street · London EC1V 9HU · 0171-505 2000

For Christmas I got my Mummy back

Shelter
CHRISTMAS
APPEAL

<u>**Will you give £19 so that homeless families,**</u>
<u>**like Tim and his Mum, can count on Shelter this Christmas?**</u>

November 1996

here bold and underlining are used to emphasise the main point of the letter.

Dear Supporter,

It's hard for me to tell you how much your donations mean to homeless people, as the nights begin drawing in, and Christmas approaches.

I'd like to tell you what you helped us do on Christmas Day for Cathy and Tim, a homeless mother and her child.

bold print and handwriting suggests informality.

On Christmas Day, at 9.30 at night, our Nightline service received a call concerning Cathy and Tim. They had been separated that day because their local council maintained that they had a responsibility to house Tim, but not his Mum.

She was distraught. It was Christmas Day. Losing her home was bad enough, but she had lost her adored little boy as well. She was left alone on the empty streets of London.

That's when Shelter is there for homeless people – when there seems to be nowhere else for them to go. Like Christmas Day.

use of italics to focus attention on a specific event, in this case Christmas Day.

Our Nightline service is open 365 days a year, and it runs 24 hours a day over the holiday period. We were there for Cathy – and were able to advise the council that, by separating a mother and her child, **they were breaking the law.**

So the council had to **immediately** reverse their decision. Cathy and Tim were reunited by the end of Christmas Day.

Getting Tim back was the best Christmas Present that I've ever had, and the only one I wanted.

Logos and slogans

Many companies and charities have their own emblem or trademark by which they can be easily identified. This is known as the **logo**. They may also use a distinctive phrase, again as a mark of identity. This is known as the **slogan**.

Illustrations

Photographs and pictures are often used to add interest and variety to a written text.

Illustrations may also enable the writer to present complex information in a simplified form.

Charts and diagrams

Particularly complex and detailed information is also often presented in the form of charts and diagrams.

ACTIVITY 2

- Can you identify Shelter's logo and slogan from the letter opposite?
- Can you think of any other well-known logos and slogans?

ACTIVITY 3

- How does the photograph in the Shelter letter relate to the subject matter?
- Do you think this letter is effectively presented? Give your reasons.

ACTIVITY 4

Look at the charts and diagrams below and on the following page. For each one decide:

- what information is being given to you
- why this information would be more difficult to explain in words without any graphics.

A

CANCER RESEARCH CAMPAIGN SUN PROTECTION LOTION

Price	£7.99/£1.40
SPF *label*	20
SPF *our tests*	27.5
UVA protection	✓
Water resistant	✓

AVON BRONZE SENSITIVE SUN LOTION

Price	£6.99/£1.22
SPF *label*	15
SPF *our tests*	20.5
UVA protection	✓
Water resistant	✓

THE BODY SHOP WATERMELON SUN LOTION

Price	£7.95 (250ml)/£1.11
SPF *label*	12
SPF *our tests*	12.6
UVA protection	✓
Water resistant	✓

BOOTS SOLTAN SUN LOTION

Price	£8.49/£1.49
SPF *label*	15
SPF *our tests*	16.8
UVA protection	✓
Water resistant	✓

BERGASOL VITAMINS A&E TANNING SUNBLOCK CREAM [1]

Price	£7.95 (75ml)/£3.71
SPF *label*	10
SPF *our tests*	14.5
UVA protection	✓
Water resistant	✓

B ►

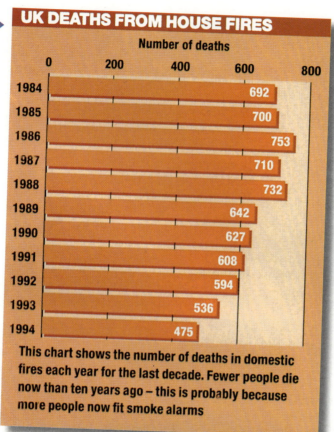

UK DEATHS FROM HOUSE FIRES

Number of deaths

Year	Number of deaths
1984	692
1985	700
1986	753
1987	710
1988	732
1989	642
1990	627
1991	608
1992	594
1993	536
1994	475

This chart shows the number of deaths in domestic fires each year for the last decade. Fewer people die now than ten years ago – this is probably because more people now fit smoke alarms

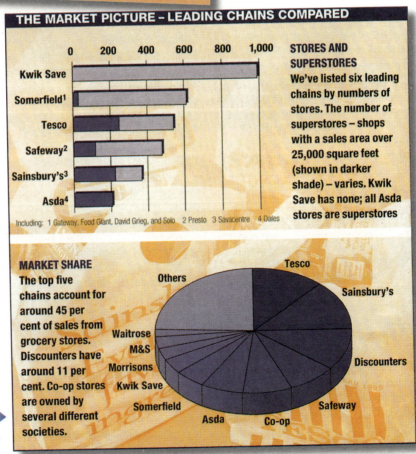

THE MARKET PICTURE – LEADING CHAINS COMPARED

Kwik Save
Somerfield[1]
Tesco
Safeway[2]
Sainsbury's[3]
Asda[4]

Including: 1 Gateway, Food Giant, David Grieg, and Solo 2 Presto 3 Savacentre 4 Dales

STORES AND SUPERSTORES
We've listed six leading chains by numbers of stores. The number of superstores – shops with a sales area over 25,000 square feet (shown in darker shade) – varies. Kwik Save has none; all Asda stores are superstores

MARKET SHARE
The top five chains account for around 45 per cent of sales from grocery stores. Discounters have around 11 per cent. Co-op stores are owned by several different societies.

Others
Tesco
Sainsbury's
Discounters
Waitrose
M&S
Morrisons
Kwik Save
Somerfield
Asda
Co-op
Safeway

C ►

Practice

ACTIVITY 5

Now look closely at the newspaper article on pages 24–25, and identify the main presentational devices:

- headings and sub-headings
- photographs and captions
- the use of bold print, underlining and italics
- the different ways in which information is conveyed to the reader.

ACTIVITY 6

Write about the main presentational devices by answering these questions.

- What use is made of headlines and sub-headings?
- In what way does the pun in the headline focus on the subject of the article?
- How do the photographs reflect the subject matter?
- Would the audience, in this case the readers of the newspaper, be familiar with the images in the photographs?
- What is the effect of the captions that accompany the photographs?
- Why is the information on the **Top 10 Violent Films** presented separately?
- Is there anything else about the presentation that you would like to comment on?
- Do you think this article is well presented? Give reasons for your answer.

Structure

The term **structure** refers to the way the ideas are organized, linked together and developed. One structural device, already discussed, is the use of sub-headings. Another is the use of paragraphs.

In the newspaper article the paragraphs are very short, generally one or two sentences in length. Why do you think it has been presented like this?

ACTIVITY 7

1 The article is about a survey and the report that followed it. Write the numbers 1 to 21 down the side of your page, one for each paragraph in the article. Write the first few words of each paragraph alongside each number.

   e.g. 1 TV chiefs come under heavy fire
         2 A survey of 200 thrillers and action movies...
         3 "We can't throw up our hands in horror

2 Go through the article carefully, making a note of which paragraphs deal with:

   - the results of the survey
   - named films
   - the recommendations of the report
   - what people say.

   A pattern should quickly emerge. The results of the survey and report are revealed gradually in the course of the article. Examples of films and quotes from relevant people or agencies are used to illustrate or provide a commentary on the results.

Gunning for TV

Survey spotlights firearms culture

TV chiefs came under fire yesterday over the amount of gun violence on our screens.

A survey of 200 thrillers and action movies shown last year revealed 835 incidents involving firearms. The National Viewers' and Listeners' Association demanded immediate action by broadcasters over the gun culture.

"We can't throw up our hands in horror over an event like the Dunblane shootings and then say there is nothing we can do about it," said general secretary John Beyer.

"Our research shows that violence is still shown on television week in, week out. There is a discrepancy between what the broadcasters say and what they actually show on TV.

"They must respond to public concern over a climate of social violence which, more and more, reflects what is shown on screen. But they are locked into a ratings war that makes them overlook their social obligations."

NVLA volunteers watched 200 films on BBC1, BBC2, ITV and Channel 4, and found that shooting was by far the most common form of violence.

Top of the trigger-happy films was Licence to Kill, starring Timothy Dalton as James Bond. It was shown on ITV at 7.50pm – more than an hour before the 9pm watershed – and contained 16 incidents involving firearms, more than Dirty Harry or Die Hard.

In addition to the 835 gun incidents in the survey, there

by PAUL GALLAGHER

were 689 occasions when actors were shown punching or kicking one another and 232 attacks involving knives.

Nearly all the films were shown after 9pm – but the survey revealed that while BBC1 is moving violent ones back in its schedules, ITV is showing them earlier.

Vamp, which features six violent assaults, two arson attacks and five knife incidents, was held back until 12.15am by BBC1 last March – four years after being screened at 9.50pm.

On the other hand, ITV brought the scheduled start times of Basic Instinct and Total Recall forward by 40 minutes so they could be shown at 10pm.

"We do not accept the argument that if films are shown at 2am it doesn't matter how

TOP 10 VIOLENT FILMS

The 10 films with the most incidents featuring firearms

MOVIE	CHANNEL	TIME	INCIDENTS
Licence to Kill	ITV	7.50pm	16
Patriot Games	BBC1	9.20pm	15
Die Hard	ITV	9.00pm	14
48 Hours	BBC2	10.20pm	14
A Town Called Hell	BBC1	1.05pm	14
The Grissom Gang	BBC1	11.40pm	14
Rock N Roll Cop	Channel 4	11.30pm	14
Dirty Harry	ITV	10.05pm	13
The Rookie	ITV	9.00pm	13
The Last Boy Scout	ITV	9.00pm	13

GUN CRAZY: Eastwood as Dirty Harry

tide of violence

much violence is in them," said Mr Beyer.

"Children have access to video recorders and they can stay up later than 9pm."

The report – More Cruelty and Violence 2 – makes a series of recommendations, including a greater priority to showing peaceful solutions to problems.

It also calls on broadcasting authorities to be "more assertive" when dealing with Hollywood by rejecting films with violent scenes, especially those involving firearms.

Yet the report revealed that some of the most successful thrillers have relatively few aggressive scenes. Fatal Attraction had only four and Jagged Edge three.

And the study also confirms that fans of violent movies need look no further than Clint Eastwood playing a cop.

His two police films Dirty Harry and The Rookie featured a total of 40 violent incidents between them, mostly involving the use of guns.

The BBC said: "We have careful guidelines on the portrayal of violence. It is an area in which we remain sensitive to public opinion, concerns and debate.

"Research shows that viewers have a very clear and widespread understanding of the watershed and the BBC takes care to ensure that programmes are adequately signposted prior to transmission."

Channel 4 and the Independent Television Commission were unavailable for comment.

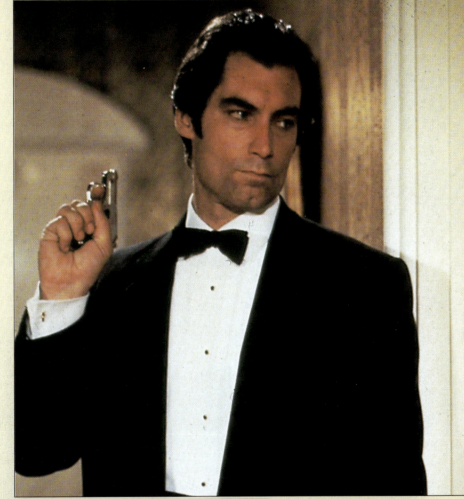

TRIGGER HAPPY: The kinds of scenes under fire for bringing too much violence to our screens. Critics say TV companies fighting a ratings war must act to curb the number of dramatic shots featuring action men like James Bond, played by Timothy Dalton, and Bruce Willis in the Die Hard movies.

Emotive language

Sometimes journalists try to influence the way the reader will react to the information they are presenting by using words or phrases that target particular emotions or anxieties. This is known as **emotive use of language**. When writing about the way information is presented you need to consider the words that are being used and the effect they are intended to have on the reader.

ACTIVITY 8

Think about the following phrases taken from the article:

- *tide of violence*
- *firearms culture*
- *gun culture*
- *a climate of social violence*
- *trigger-happy films*

What is their effect **a)** individually and **b)** collectively?

Why do you think the writer used language in this way?

POINTS to remember

- Headlines are designed to capture the reader's interest.
- Sub-headings and paragraphs are a means of organizing ideas.
- Bold print, italics, underlining, captions, logos and slogans are all presentational devices.
- Emotive language is used to persuade the reader of a particular point of view.

Follow an argument

A writer may develop an argument in favour of banning violent films on TV. Another may argue that all children should stay at school until the age of seventeen. Yet another may argue that all cigarette advertising should be banned. To construct an argument the writer must develop his/her point of view and will probably draw on factual evidence and the opinions of others to support this.

In the article on TV violence in the previous section the writer argued, using statistical evidence, that there was too much violence on TV. It is important to remember, however, that although an argument may refer to factual evidence it is, nevertheless, based on opinion. In order to follow an argument you need to be able to identify the key points that the writer is making.

THE BELLS, THE BELLS!

ROGER ST PIERRE gives audible warning of new ideas for canalside cyclists

Ting-a-ling-a-ling! Time was when it was deemed obligatory to have a bell on your bike. That was before, somewhere in the Fifties and after a long fight, the cycling lobby managed to win their argument that a shouted warning of "Oi! Get out of the way!" qualified as the Road Traffic Act's requisite 'audible warning of approach'.

Though manufacturers continued to supply a bell with each new bike they old – somewhere separately in the cardboard bike box and usually destined to be thrown out with the wrappings – to all intents bicycle bells went the way of cycle clips.

The arguments had been cogent: than the human voice carries further than any bicycle bell – though not as far as an electrically powered air horn! – and that, in any event, fingers grabbing for the bell would be better used grabbing for the brakes.

End of story ... or so we thought. Now, however, well over three decades later there are people who would like cycle bell manufacturers to get back into business (I hope they'll produce those natty little numbers in glitzy anodised finishes rather than drab aluminium or plain chrome!)

It seems that walkers, anglers and everyman and his dog wants bikies to (a) be more considerate (fair enough) and (b) to unfailingly give warning of imminent approach (though I guess, before too long they'll be complaining just as stridently about being disturbed by all the resultant noise).

Those who have toured extensively on the Continent will know that, in some countries, it has long been the custom for motorists coming up behind cyclists on the road to give a warning toot of their horn – not as an aggressive gesture of "Damn it, get out of my way!" but as a simple courtesy to warn that they are about to overtake. Of course, many first-timers from the UK have taken this the wrong way and complained of being harassed but you soon get used to local customs.

Take riding on the wrong, well right, side of the road. It's a little known fact – as Michael Caine might put it – that there are still almost as many countries which follow our lead and drive on the left (Australia, Japan, Indonesia to name just three ..) as follow Napo...... ...ction to keep to the right...

copy of the 1903 RAC Conti..... according to which the rule .... on the right on country road..... and then switch back to the..... probably explains why most..... middle of the road.

Anyway, back to the bells.

Water.... .... pos ..... ch ..... th ..... the ..... fully ..... taxatio..... when pu..... mission ..... The a..... to glide ..... to fish in ..... pay for t..... especially ..... to up ke..... say that ..... should l..... especially ..... them th.....

The is..... charging ..... practica..... brings t..... being p..... carrying ..... licence ..... issued ..... for the ..... paid an..... other c..... warning .....

Nob..... happen..... idea – ..... with a ..... with th..... sanctio.....

p..... bec..... comp..... it seems ..... pedestria..... who allow th..... – and there is ..... licence too.

The arguments had been cogent: that the human voice carries further than any bicycle bell – though not as far as an electrically powered air horn!

The school system that gives girls an advantage

Examination evidence shows that girls are outpacing boys. What are we to make of this? The easy answer is to accept the feminist claim that girls would always equal or surpass boys when the education system was rid of its 'male bias'. But things are not that simple. Nor that trivial.

As it happens, the results do reflect the impact of woolly educational thinking, which has played down actual examinations and elevated classroom performance through coursework. This gives girls an advantage, since their greater keenness and biddability tend to earn them higher marks than more naturally rebellious and individualistic boys.

It is not a question of begrudging girls their success. To do so would be unfair and stupid. But society is best served when the ...rity of boys are able to emerge from eleven years of ..... with the emotional and intellectual ...ingful jobs and roles. ...ly breakdown, absent fathers, the corrupt- ...dependency – are already helping to create a ...i jobless young men who prey on society. ... muggers and car thieves whose activities do ... our quality of life. The 'feminization' of the ...s prizes-for-all ethos, will simply push more ...hool.

...ar it for the girls. They have done what was ... – and well. But if there is not a return to tests ...pil to show what he or she has in his head, we ...ing *from* the boys. And we shall not like what

Riders claim doping rife at the top

DOPING has become commonplace among professional riders in recent years, involving most of the sport's top 50, according to two recently retired riders.

Gilles Delion, who stopped riding at the end of last season, said in an article in the French sports daily L'Equipe that a French team director told him that "you couldn't be among the world's best 50 riders if you didn't take EPO, and it's been that way for quite a while."

EPO (erythropoietin) is a performance-enhancing substance that stimulates the production of red blood cells which transport oxygen around the body. All French teams are now involved in doping, Delion claimed.

Delion, regarded as a highly promising rider who never quite reached the very top, despite winning the Tour of Lombardy in 1990 and a stage of the 1992 Tour de France, said he saw riders looking for ice cubes in hotels to keep the vials containing EPO cool.

"I also saw a rider take EPO," he said. "I wasn't shocked because I knew such things happened but usually the riders would lock themselves up in the bathroom."

Nicolas Aubier, who retired at the end of last season because he felt the sport had been debased by doping, said he was forced to use prohibited substances. "Frankly I can't imagine a rider belonging to the top 100 and not taking EPO, growth hormones or another product," he told L'Equipe. "The problem is that the use of doping products has become so general that anybody not taking anything is regarded as abnormal."

Real People Real Training

By Gordon Styles*

*H*as anybody else out there noticed how long it takes a garage technician to remove a radio from the average car. Certainly when you get the bill it's never less than half an hour.

Has anybody noticed how long it takes a 13 year old car thief – probably less than a few minutes including a preplanned escape – and he (she) didn't even need the keys! They could also drive the car away in the same amount of time. OK – I'm being cynical and no offence is meant to self respecting garage technicians, at least they don't rip out half the dash board as well.

The point is that a so called 'car thief' is by no means unable to pick up what they consider to be very useful skills and carry out a 'complex' operation very quickly. What is their motivation to do this? They get excitement, money and adulation from peers.

It just so happens that the brain is inseparable from the body. For millions of years man has always used the brain and the body in equal amounts – we had to in order for us to survive as a species. So why in the twentieth century did we decide, in our wisdom, that we should teach children to only use the brain and very often the use of the body was frowned upon. Most children are unable to use the brain without somehow engaging the body at the same time. Most children's brains are creating chemicals designed to stimulate the body, and if you don't let the kid use its body you have got one very physically or emotionally frustrated youngster on your hands. This is not an 'excuse' for socially unacceptable behaviour, but it could be a contributing factor.

*I*n every problem there is an opportunity. The UK presently has the biggest industrial skills shortage in history.

We as a country desperately need to grow our manufacturing industries but we have a four or five year delay going on because we can't find enough skilled people. So what is the opportunity? I believe it is time to flip the schooling system on its head. Seeing as less than 10% of children are pure academics we should take all the children out of school at the age of 13 and send them for one year to a proper traditionally run apprentice school at which they would be engaged in learning real physical skills that are of use in our modern industrial society. Those who are obviously not cut out for physical work, probably 15% to 25% of children, could then ask to be sent to 'special' schools that are set up to deal very specifically with Academics, Artists, Musicians, Dancers, etc. These kids will now be in the correct environment for their talents and will probably excel beyond normal expectations.

The rest of them spend a further 3 years going through a 'traditional' apprenticeship covering all things physical, mechanical and electrical. 'My' kind of apprenticeship would be fun and you get paid! £35 a week may not sound like much to you but to a kid of 13, it's enough to give the motivation to learn. These wages would come from industry in the form of contracts as part of their training.

I want to see all the disciplines within mechanical and electrical engineering being taught. I would expect to see relevant academic studies such as mathematics, physics and history being taught alongside the physical training and preferably on the workshop floor. e.g. How does the internal combustion engine work? who invented it? and how to calculate the gearing ratios in the gear box? Some might ask - what about the academically challenged, as the politically correct would have them referred to. Surely these children are the ones who need to learn physical skills most. A scheme of this kind would encourage all children and ultimately bene..ts

Identify key points

Read the magazine article opposite, in which Gordon Styles argues for a change in the current education system.

To understand the argument you need to identify the main points that the writer is making. It helps to divide the argument into two stages, as in the article itself. Here are the main points of the first stage:

Stage 1

- It takes a thirteen-year-old car thief less time to steal a car than it takes a garage mechanic to remove a radio from one.
- A car thief has the ability to learn a 'complex' operation quickly.
- They learn the 'skill' because they are highly motivated.
- Twentieth-century education concentrates on development of the brain at the expense of the body.
- Most children become frustrated if they are not allowed to use their bodies.

ACTIVITY 1

Now list the main points of Stage 2 of the argument.

Identify implications and inconsistencies

Once you have been able to identify the main strands of a particular argument, you are ready to assess the value of the argument itself and to identify its implications.

ACTIVITY 2

Think about the *Real People Real Training* article again and answer the following questions:

- Do children break into cars because they are not motivated at school?
- Would most children be happier and more fulfilled on an apprenticeship of the type described? Would you?
- Is it realistic to expect industry to fund this scheme?
- Would parents be happy with it? If not, why not?
- What would happen to children who experience difficulty or don't conform?
- If children are involved in manufacturing goods will this create unemployment amongst adults?
- Should education be dictated solely by the needs of industry?

By answering questions of this kind you are starting to develop your own point of view on a subject you had probably not considered before. As a reader, it is important that you should question what you read and form your own opinions on it.

Real People Real Training

By Gordon Styles*

***H**as anybody else out there noticed how long it takes a garage technician to remove a radio from the average car? Certainly when you get the bill it's never less than half an hour.*

Has anybody noticed how long it takes a 13 year old car thief – probably less than a few minutes including a preplanned escape – and he (she) didn't even need the keys! They could also drive the car away in the same amount of time. OK - I'm being cynical and no offence is meant to self respecting garage technicians, at least they don't rip out half the dash board as well.

The point is that a so called 'car thief' is by no means unable to pick up what they consider to be very useful skills and carry out a 'complex' operation very quickly. What is their motivation to do this? They get excitement, money and adulation from peers.

It just so happens that the brain is inseparable from the body. For millions of years man has always used the brain and the body in equal amounts – we had to in order for us to survive as a species. So why in the twentieth century did we decide, in our wisdom, that we should teach children to only use the brain and very often the use of the body was frowned upon? Most children are unable to use the brain without somehow engaging the body at the same time. Most children's brains are creating chemicals designed to stimulate the body, and if you don't let the kid use its body you have got one very physically or emotionally frustrated youngster on your hands. This is not an 'excuse' for socially unacceptable behaviour, but it could be a contributing factor.

***I**n every problem there is an opportunity. The UK presently has the biggest industrial skills shortage in history.*

We as a country desperately need to grow our manufacturing industries but we have a four or five year delay going on because we can't find enough skilled people. So what is the opportunity? I believe it is time to flip the schooling system on its head. Seeing as less than 10% of children are pure academics we should take all the children out of school at the age of 13 and send them for one year to a proper traditionally run apprentice school at which they would be engaged in learning real physical skills that are of use in our modern industrial society. Those who are obviously not cut out for physical work, probably 15% to 25% of children, could then ask to be sent to 'special' schools that are set up to deal very specifically with Academics, Artists, Musicians, Dancers, etc. These kids will now be in the correct environment for their talents and will probably excel beyond normal expectations.

The rest of them spend a further 3 years going through a 'traditional' apprenticeship covering all things physical, mechanical and electrical. 'My' kind of apprenticeship would be fun and you get paid! £35 a week may not sound like much to you but to a kid of 13, it's enough to give the motivation to learn. These wages would come from industry in the form of contracts as part of their training.

I want to see all the disciplines within mechanical and electrical engineering being taught. I would expect to see relevant academic studies such as mathematics, physics and history being taught alongside the physical training and preferably on the workshop floor. e.g. How does the internal combustion engine work? who invented it? and how to calculate the gearing ratios in the gear box? Some might ask - what about the academically challenged, as the politically correct would have them referred to? Surely these children are the ones who need to learn physical skills most. A scheme of this kind would encourage all children and ultimately benefit society as a whole. Tell me who is more important to the UK's financial well being – a world class labourer or a no class politician?

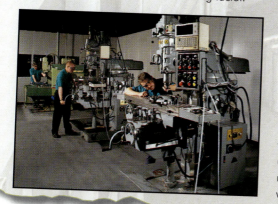

*Teeside Business Executive of the Year 1996, Managing Director of Styles Precision Components Limited.

Practice

Read the following editorial which was written in response to the evidence that girls were achieving more at school than boys. As you read it make notes on the main stages of the argument.

The school system that gives girls an advantage

Examination evidence shows that girls are outpacing boys. What are we to make of this? The easy answer is to accept the feminist claim that girls would always equal or surpass boys when the education system was rid of its 'male bias'. But things are not that simple. Nor that trivial.

As it happens, the results do reflect the impact of woolly educational thinking, which has played down actual examinations and elevated classroom performance through coursework. This gives girls an advantage, since their greater keenness and biddability tend to earn them higher marks than more naturally rebellious and individualistic boys.

It is not a question of begrudging girls their success. To do so would be unfair and stupid. But society is best served when the great majority of boys are able to emerge from eleven years of compulsory schooling with the emotional and intellectual equipment to find meaningful jobs and roles.

Other factors – family breakdown, absent fathers, the corrupting effects of welfare dependency – are already helping to create a pool of anti-social and jobless young men who prey on society. These are the burglars, muggers and car thieves whose activities do so much to drag down our quality of life. The 'feminization' of the school system, with its prizes-for-all ethos, will simply push more young men into this pool.

So, yes, let us hear it for the girls. They have done what was demanded of them – and well. But if there is not a return to tests which challenge a pupil to show what he or she has in his head, we shall surely be hearing *from* the boys. And we shall not like what we hear.

THE DAILY EXPRESS

ACTIVITY 3

Now answer the following questions on the article opposite:

- What image is given of **a)** girls and **b)** boys?
- Can you find particular words and phrases which help to convey these images to the reader?
- What factors are seen as affecting boys' achievements?
- Are these factors seen as affecting girls' achievements in the same way?
- What facts are contained within this editorial?
- What is the writer hoping to achieve?
- Are there any ideas in it that you would want to challenge or question? If so, what are they?

ACTIVITY 4

You have the opportunity to write a letter responding to the views expressed in the editorial.

- List the key points you would want to include in your letter.
- Organize them into the most appropriate order.

POINTS to remember

- An argument is usually based on a mixture of fact and opinion.
- To understand the argument you need to identify the main points that the writer is making.
- You should always question what you read and be prepared to form your own opinions on it.

What **type** of text is this?

How did you decide?

Generally you can identify an advertisement just by looking at it. You don't need to read it to know **what** it is. The same is true of many other types of texts. We make judgements about them very quickly based on their appearance.

ACTIVITY 1

Look at each of the following five texts A–E but do not read them. For each one decide:

- what kind of text it is
- where you might find it
- who it is written for
- what it is about.

Once you have decided, try to explain what evidence led you to the decisions you made. Were some more difficult than others? If so, why?

The Josephine & John Bowes Museum

presents

Fashions in Jane Austen's Time

See the costumes as worn by

Jennifer Ehle
Emma Thompson
Kate Winslet
Alan Rickman
Colin Firth

in a new and exciting exhibition of costumes from the recent Emma Thompson film 'Sense and Sensibility' and the BBC TV production of 'Pride and Prejudice'

plus

original, early 19th century costumes from the Museum's own collection.

A

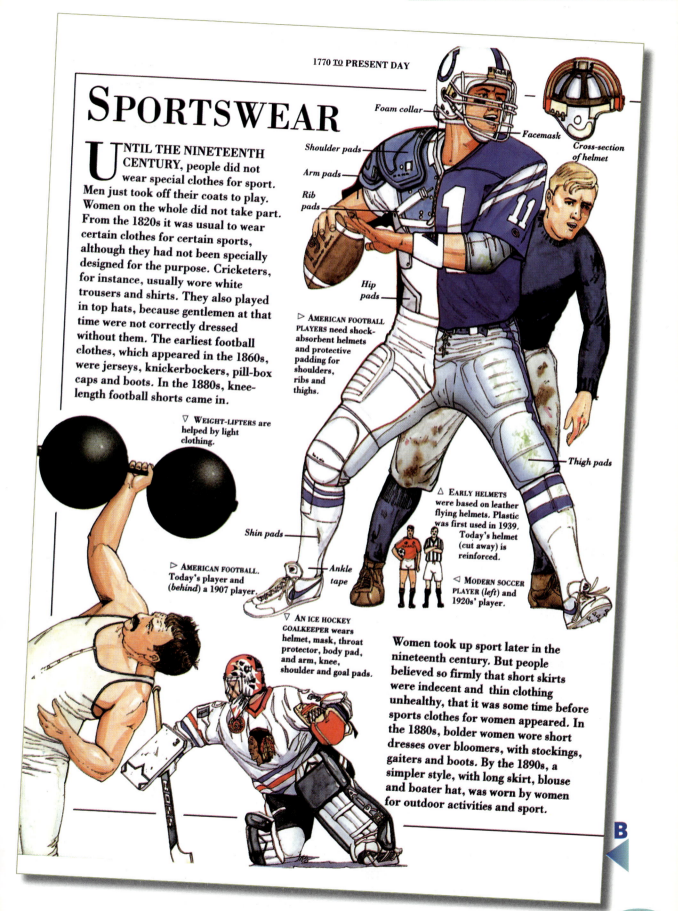

1770 TO PRESENT DAY

SPORTSWEAR

UNTIL THE NINETEENTH CENTURY, people did not wear special clothes for sport. Men just took off their coats to play. Women on the whole did not take part. From the 1820s it was usual to wear certain clothes for certain sports, although they had not been specially designed for the purpose. Cricketers, for instance, usually wore white trousers and shirts. They also played in top hats, because gentlemen at that time were not correctly dressed without them. The earliest football clothes, which appeared in the 1860s, were jerseys, knickerbockers, pill-box caps and boots. In the 1880s, knee-length football shorts came in.

Foam collar

Shoulder pads

Arm pads

Rib pads

Hip pads

Facemask

Cross-section of helmet

Thigh pads

Shin pads

Ankle tape

▷ AMERICAN FOOTBALL PLAYERS need shock-absorbent helmets and protective padding for shoulders, ribs and thighs.

▽ WEIGHT-LIFTERS are helped by light clothing.

△ EARLY HELMETS were based on leather flying helmets. Plastic was first used in 1939. Today's helmet (cut away) is reinforced.

◁ MODERN SOCCER PLAYER (left) and 1920s' player.

▷ AMERICAN FOOTBALL. Today's player and (behind) a 1907 player.

▽ AN ICE HOCKEY GOALKEEPER wears helmet, mask, throat protector, body pad, and arm, knee, shoulder and goal pads.

Women took up sport later in the nineteenth century. But people believed so firmly that short skirts were indecent and thin clothing unhealthy, that it was some time before sports clothes for women appeared. In the 1880s, bolder women wore short dresses over bloomers, with stockings, gaiters and boots. By the 1890s, a simpler style, with long skirt, blouse and boater hat, was worn by women for outdoor activities and sport.

B

dilemmas Virginia Ironside

THIS WEEK'S PROBLEM:
Marina has a problem with her children's appearances. Her 14-year-old son is planning to get a ring through his nose, with or without his parent's permission; her 12-year-old daughter wears mini-skirts so short her bottom shows. Marina wants to give them their freedom but she doesn't know how far she should go

Adolescent children are fantastically self-conscious about their appearance. They'll wear nothing that isn't dead right for their crowd. That's why, if you buy them a green jersey of the wrong green, or a pair of socks covered with musical notes that you think are "fun" and they think are naff, they often simply refuse to wear them.

So when Marina's children decide to take certain design decisions, she can be certain that in their own circle they'll look absolutely spot on. She may think they look weird; their friends will think they look the bee's knees.

The fact that *she* thinks they look provocative or brutal is beside the point. Who cares what adults think? A gang of skinheads is hardly likely to pounce on a boy just because of a ring in his nose; they'll have far more sympathy with Marina's young son that Marina herself. Little girls who show their bums in the street may get wolf-whistles and leery looks, but rapists' victims, if newspaper pictures are anything to go by, are more likely to be wearing trackie bottoms or school uniforms than revealing little numbers.

In the sixties, I was one of the first to wear mini-skirts, long black boots and fish-net stockings. The look shrieked "tart" in a far louder voice then than any mini-skirt from Jigsaw would today. Nothing ever happened to me because of my clothes.

Marina must remember not only her own teenage whims but also how irritating it was when her children begged her not to wear certain things to pick them up from school. "Oh, Mum, you look so weird in those funny trousers ..." was the wail from my son when I went a bit mad on some ghastly, never-to-be-worn-again breeches.

But as we, as parents, tone down our dress when in the company of our children and their friends to save them dreadful embarrassment, it's quite right that our children should do the same when around our contemporaries – or their grandparents. Longer skirts. Nose-ring temporarily removed. But, generally, dress is a harmless way of expressing individuality. If Marina forces her kids into V-necked jumpers and clean jeans, their individuality will only express itself in other, far more dangerous ways. Neat as pins on the outside; probably stoned to the eyebrows on the inside.

Marina can express her anxieties, but after that she should shut up as she starts to practise the difficult new "hands-off" parenting of the adolescent. "It's only a phase," she can remind herself. Only too soon, sadly, her children are going to look pretty much exactly the same as all the other young men and women in the street.

fash+ion ('fæʃən) n. **1. a.** style in clothes, cosmetics, behaviour, etc., esp. the latest or most admired style. **b.** (as modifier): fashion magazine. **2. a.** manner of performance; mode; way: a striking fashion. **b.** (in combination): crab-fashion. **3.** a way of life that revolves around the activities, dress, interests, etc. that are most fashionable. **4.** shape, appearance, or form. **5.** sort; kind; type. **6. after** or **in a fashion. a.** in some manner, but not very well: I mended it, after a fashion. **b.** of a low order, of a sort: he is a poet, after a fashion. **7. after the fashion of.** like, similar to. **8. of fashion.** of high social standing. ~vb. (tr.) to give a particular form to. **10.** to make suitable or fitting. **11.** Obsolete. to contrive; manage. [C13 facioun form, manner from Old French faceon, from Latin factiō a making, from facere to make] — 'fash+ion+er n.

D

Miss S.'s daily emergence from the van was highly dramatic. Suddenly and without warning the rear door would be flung open to reveal the tattered draperies that masked the terrible interior. There was a pause, then through the veils would be hurled several bulging plastic sacks. Another pause, before slowly and with great caution one sturdy slippered leg came feeling for the floor before the other followed and one had the first sight of the day's wardrobe. Hats were always a feature: a black railwayman's hat with a long neb worn slightly on the skew so that she looked like a drunken signalman or a French guardsman of the 1880s; there was her Charlie Brown pitcher's hat; and in June 1977 an octagonal straw table-mat, tied on with a chiffon scarf and a bit of cardboard for the peak. She also went in for green eyeshades. Her skirts had a telescopic appearance, as they had often been lengthened many times over by the simple expedient of sewing a strip of extra cloth around the hem, though with no attempt at matching. One skirt was made by sewing several orange dusters together. When she fell foul of authority she put it down to her clothes. Once, late at night, the police rang me from Tunbridge Wells. They had picked her up on the station, thinking her dress was a nightie. She was indignant. 'Does it look like a nightie? You see lots of people wearing dresses like this. I don't think this style can have got to Tunbridge Wells yet.'

WRITING HOME BY ALAN BENNETT

E

Scanning

As well as making judgements on the nature of a particular text, based on its appearance, we are also able to extract information from a text quickly.

When you select what TV programmes you want to watch over Christmas it is unlikely that you read every single detail on every programme listed in the TV guide. You probably **scan** each day's programmes and make your selection very quickly, without actually realizing that you are using quite an advanced reading skill to do so. When you need to find particular facts or details you don't usually read the entire text. Your eyes move quickly over the surface until they focus on the information you are looking for.

ACTIVITY 2

See how quickly you can *scan* the texts on pages 32–5. Make a record of how long it takes you to find the answers to the following questions:

- What were the earliest football clothes?
- What kind of hats did Miss S. wear?
- Where could you go to find out more about fashions in Jane Austen's time?
- What problem does Marina have with her children?
- Why did it take some time for sports clothes for women to appear?
- Whose son complained that she looked weird 'in those funny trousers'?
- What is meant by the phrase 'after the fashion of'?

Skimming

In Activity 2 you were **scanning** the texts in order to find particular details. Once you found them you presumably stopped reading the text. Sometimes we need to read the whole of a text quickly in order to get a general idea of what it is about. This is known as **skim-reading**.

ACTIVITY 3

Practise your skills in skim-reading. Decide, as quickly as you can, which text(s), or part of text(s), you would select to help you answer questions on the following subjects:

- early sportswear
- women and clothes
- the changing face of fashion
- clothing as an expression of personal individuality.

Which text would give you most facts about clothing? Which text relies most heavily on opinion?

POINTS to remember

- It is possible to identify many different types of text by their appearance.
- We **scan** a text in order to find a particular detail.
- We **skim** a text in order to get a general idea of what it is about.

Collate material from different sources

Sometimes you will be asked questions that require you to examine and write about texts or parts of texts in some detail. You may be asked to use material from them in order to build a wider picture or to note points of agreement and disagreement between them.

In order to achieve this you need to be able to take different pieces of information from different texts and use them together. To do this you will need to make notes, and your skills in scanning and skim-reading a text will be very important.

Making notes

We all have our own way of making notes and our method changes, and hopefully improves, the more practice we have. The important thing to remember about making notes is that it should not take too long and that the notes should be suited to the purpose for which they are needed.

If you are asked to make notes on a particular character in a story you are reading you may be expected to write in complete sentences so that your teacher can understand what you mean. In an exam situation it is different. You are the only person who will read your notes so there is no need to write in sentences. Short phrases or bullet points should be adequate.

ACTIVITY 1

Look at **Text B** (page 33) on Sportswear again. Your notes could be written

Text B - probably encyclopedia or reference - uses illustration
special clothes for sport introduced in 19th century
men's clothes for cricket and football were first - details given
some changes for women in the 1880s and 90s
details of contemporary American Football outfit
1907 player shown in contrast
weight-lifter and ice hockey goalkeeper also shown

You may even find a shorter route by using common abbreviations for words, e.g. prob. for probably or illus. for illustration.

Now make your own notes on Texts A to E (pages 32–35).

ACTIVITY 2

What did you learn from these articles about clothes and fashion?

In order for you to answer this question successfully, you need to draw information together from each of the different extracts. Here are some useful linking points for you to consider.

1 Clothes change over time and according to need.

Text A

Text B

2 Clothes are an expression of individuality.

Text C

Text E

3 Fashion affects people's attitudes to clothes and other people.

Text A

Text C

Text D

Try to think of other ways in which these texts could be linked before gathering your information and starting to write.

POINTS *to remember*

- To collate information you need to take details from different texts and use them together.

- Notes should always be adapted to the purpose for which they are required.

How to approach Paper 1 Section A

Now that you have revised the skills you need for Paper 1 Section A you can start looking at the types of examination questions you are likely to come across. Remember that the source materials for this section will include all kinds of factual materials which may be extracts from autobiographies, biographies, journals, diaries, travel writing, leaflets, newspaper articles, factual and informative materials. You will have at least two different sources to look at. The more familiar you are with materials of this kind before the exam, the easier you will find it.

You are allowed one hour for this section of the question paper. Spend about ten minutes reading through the questions and the source materials.

Answering the questions

The questions are placed at the **beginning** of the section in the examination paper so that you know what you are being asked to do before you read the text(s). It is very important that you read these questions carefully and take time to work out exactly what you are being asked to do. Break the questions down into separate parts and construct a brief answer plan.

Here is an example of the type of question you might be asked:

> The writers of the two extracts present different points of view. Which do you think is most likely to persuade the reader, and why?
>
> In your answer you should consider the following:
> * content   * layout   * language.

The first sentence is a statement about two extracts. The second is the question you have to address and the third is telling you how to do it. On the basis of this you can make a short answer plan:

Paragraph 1 – compare content of both extracts
Paragraph 2 – compare layout of both extracts
Paragraph 3 – compare language features of both extracts
Paragraph 4 – say which is the most effective using points covered in paragraphs 1–3 as evidence.

On the following pages you will find two sample Section A papers, one for Foundation Tier and one for Higher. Your teacher will tell you which one you should work on. Each section is followed by a breakdown of the questions and advice on how you should answer them. Work through this section carefully and only attempt to answer the questions when you have read and understood the advice and completed any preliminary tasks.

Exam Practice – Foundation Tier

PAPER 1 SECTION A

- Read the letter **Edinburgh, My Hometown**, the tourist information leaflet **Edinburgh, So Much to See and Do**, and the travel writing extract **Edinburgh**. Answer *all* parts of the question that follows.
- Spend *about one hour* on this section.

1   a)   i List *three* opinions in **Edinburgh, My Hometown**.

               ii List *three* facts in the first paragraph of **Edinburgh, So Much to See and Do**.

        b)   What points does Bill Bryson make in **Edinburgh** to support his view that it is an exciting and different place?

        c)   All *three* pieces suggest that Edinburgh is a place worth visiting.

               Compare *two* of these, explaining which you found to be the most effective and why.

               You should comment on:

                 i what they are about

                 ii the way the information is presented

                 iii the way the writers use language

                 iv similarities and/or differences between the pieces

                 v your own response to the pieces.

My HOME TOWN

EDINBURGH

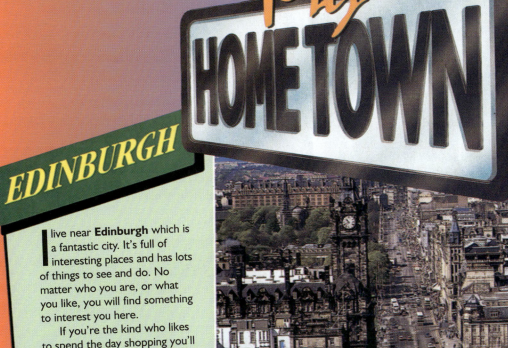

I live near **Edinburgh** which is a fantastic city. It's full of interesting places and has lots of things to see and do. No matter who you are, or what you like, you will find something to interest you here.

If you're the kind who likes to spend the day shopping you'll really enjoy a visit to **Princes Street**. Whether it's clothes, music or books that you're looking for you're sure to find them here . . . and much more. Cross the road and you come to **Waverley Market** which has something for everyone.

When you get tired of spending your money you can wander into **Princes Street Gardens** and admire the flowers or go to the top of the **Scott** monument for only £1. If the top seems too far away you can stop off at the first level and still enjoy the views. There's always lots of people around and in the summer, particularly during the **Festival**, the whole place is buzzing with life and excitement.

Those of you who are interested in sport will love Edinburgh. The **Commonwealth pool** is amazing! You can spend your time swimming or just zooming down the amazing flumes. If your nerves are weak avoid the Stingray! For the really sporty types I can highly recommend a trip to **Marco's Leisure Centre**. There's lots to do here and you'll come out feeling great . . . and exhausted.

Alternatively you could test your skating skills at the **Murrayfield ice rink** or even go and see a game of rugby at Murrayfield. On a good day you'll get to see the Scots coming out on top!

For those of you who like the quiet life, or just want a few minutes away from it all, there's the **botanical gardens**. You can spend ages just wandering and looking. If you're the friendly sort the squirrels might come over to say hello and a few slices of bread is all you'll need to entice the pigeons to eat out of your hand. Once you've had enough of the local wildlife you can turn your attention to Edinburgh's amazing history with no better place to learn than at the **Castle** itself.

After an exhausting day you'll want somewhere to relax. Edinburgh's got loads of theatres and cinemas so you won't be short of somewhere to go in the evening. I hope you make it here some day and then maybe you'll grow to love it just as much as I do.

EDINBURGH

SO MUCH TO SEE AND DO

Dominating Edinburgh's breathtaking skylines, *Edinburgh Castle* receives over one million visitors in a year. Within its ancient battlements you can see the Crown Jewels of Scotland, the Scottish National War Memorial and the tiny St Margaret's Chapel, the oldest building in Edinburgh (*circa 1090*). *The Scottish United Services Museum* at the Castle, illustrates the history of the armed forces in Scotland with displays of weapons, uniforms, equipment, orders and medals.

The Royal Botanic Garden is open all year round and provides the perfect setting for a leisurely stroll surrounded by rare and beautiful plants from all over the world.

Open to the public every day of the year, *Edinburgh Zoo* is one of the UK's largest zoological parks and makes a great day out. The recently constructed Penguin House with its underwater viewing and video displays is the largest in the world.

The Royal Museum of Scotland in Chambers Street features exhibits from around the world with particular emphasis on natural history, industry and science. Out at Ingliston, by Edinburgh Airport, the *Scottish Agricultural Museum* illustrates the life and work of Scotland's countryside over the last two centuries.

Edinburgh – "The Athens of the North" – is a city rich in art. *The National Gallery of Scotland* at the foot of the Mound features masterpieces of European art from Renaissance to Post Impressionism. Major figures from Scotland's past are captured on canvas at *The Scottish National Portrait Gallery* while the *National Gallery of Modern Art* hosts the finest collection of twentieth century art and sculpture in Scotland, in fine surroundings on the edge of the city centre. *The Royal Scottish Academy*, also on the Mound is acknowledged as one of the foremost exhibitors of contemporary art in Scotland. Their Annual Exhibition is an important event in the Scottish Arts Calendar.

The Palace of Holyroodhouse – The Queen's official residence in Scotland – is also well worth a visit. Like Edinburgh Castle, guided tours are conducted throughout the year (except when the Royal Family is in residence). The Palace was the venue for talks when Edinburgh was proud host to the European Council in December 1992.

The Museum of Childhood, perhaps the noisiest museum in the world, is just one of four fascinating local authority-owned museums on the historic Royal Mile, to which entry is free. Another of them, *The People's Story*, tells of the life and work of ordinary people in Edinburgh from the late 18th century to the present day.

John Knox's House in the High Street is an outstanding remnant from Edinburgh's medieval past. The house is associated with both James Mossman-Goldsmith to Mary Queen of Scots and John Knox, Scotland's religious reformer.

At the *Edinburgh Butterfly and Insect World*, exotic butterflies flutter by, enjoying a carefully created tropical habitat. Wildlife of a marine variety can be seen from a "diver's eye view" at the new and exciting *Deep Sea World* at North Queensferry.

EDINBURGH AND SCOTLAND INFORMATION CENTRE
Tel 0131 557 1700, 3 Princes Street, Edinburgh
– Your first call in Edinburgh

ESSENTIAL GUIDE TO EDINBURGH

EDINBURGH

And so I went to Edinburgh. Can there anywhere be a more beautiful and beguiling city to arrive at by train early on a crisp, dark Novembery evening? To emerge from Waverley Station and find yourself in the very heart of such a glorious city is a happy experience indeed. I hadn't been to Edinburgh for years and had forgotten just how captivating it can be. Every monument was lit with golden floodlights – the castle and Bank of Scotland headquarters on the hill, the Balmoral Hotel and the Scott Memorial down below – which gave them a certain eerie grandeur. The city was abustle with end-of-day activity. Buses swept through Princes Street and shop and office workers scurried along pavements, hastening home to have their haggis and cock-a-leekie soup and indulge in a few skirls or whatever it is Scots do when the sun goes doon.

I'd booked a room in the Caledonian Hotel, which was a rash and extravagant thing to do, so I set off for it down Princes Street, past the Gothic rocket ship of the Scott Memorial, unexpectedly exhilarated to find myself among the hurrying throngs and the sight of the castle on its craggy mount outlined against a pale evening sky.

To a surprising extent, and far more than in Wales, Edinburgh felt like a different country. The buildings were thin and tall in an un-English fashion, the money was different, even the air and light felt different in some ineffable northern way. Every bookshop window was full of books about Scotland or by Scottish authors. And of course the voices were different. I walked along, feeling as if I had left England far behind, and then I would pass something familiar and think in surprise, 'Oh, look, they have Marks & Spencer here,' as if I were in Reykjavik or Stavanger and oughtn't to expect to find British things. It was most refreshing.

I checked into the Caledonian, dumped my things in the room, and immediately returned to the streets, eager to be out in the open air and to take in whatever Edinburgh had to offer. I trudged up a long, curving back hill to the castle, but the grounds were shut for the night, so I contented myself with a shuffling amble down the Royal Mile, which was nearly empty of life and very handsome in a dour, Scottish sort of way.

NOTES FROM A SMALL ISLAND BY BILL BRYSON

The examiner comments...

Question 1 a) asks you to:

> i List *three* opinions in **Edinburgh, My Hometown**.
> ii List *three* facts in the first paragraph of **Edinburgh, So Much to See and Do**.

Here you are being tested on your ability to tell the difference between fact and opinion and on your ability to select material according to purpose.

Part i asks you to choose three opinions from the letter about Edinburgh. Remember that an opinion is a point of view, something which can't be proved. In this letter the writer expresses many opinions but these are often mixed up with facts about her home town. It is your task to separate them and list the opinions only. The first example of this is in the very first sentence:

> I live near **Edinburgh** which is a fantastic city.

The first part of this sentence, *I live near Edinburgh*, is **fact** but the second part is expressing the **opinion** that Edinburgh is a fantastic city.

Therefore the first opinion you could list would be:

a) i Edinburgh is a fantastic city.

Now list two more opinions that appear in the letter.

Part ii asks you to select three facts from the tourist information sheet on Edinburgh. You are asked to look at the first paragraph only.

As with the letter, this passage also contains fact and opinions and you have to separate them. Look at the first sentence:

> Dominating Edinburgh's breathtaking skylines, *Edinburgh Castle* receives over one million visitors in a year.

It is **opinion** that the castle dominates Edinburgh's breathtaking skylines but it is **fact** that it receives over one million visitors a year.

Therefore the first fact you could list would be:‹

a) ii Edinburgh Castle receives over one million visitors a year.

Now list two more facts that appear in the paragraph.

Question **1** b) asks you:

What points does Bill Bryson make in **Edinburgh** to support his view that Edinburgh is an exciting and different place?

Here you are being tested on your ability to follow an argument and to select appropriate detail.

Look at the first paragraph of the extract:

And so I went to Edinburgh. Can there anywhere be a more beautiful and beguiling city to arrive at by train early on a crisp, dark Novembery evening? To emerge from Waverley Station and find yourself in the very heart of such a glorious city is a happy experience indeed. I hadn't been to Edinburgh for years and had forgotten just how captivating it can be. Every monument was lit with golden floodlights – the castle and Bank of Scotland headquarters on the hill, the Balmoral Hotel and the Scott Memorial down below – which gave them a certain eerie grandeur. The city was abustle with end-of-day activity. Buses swept through Princes Street and shop and office workers scurried along pavements, hastening home to have their haggis and cock-a-leekie soup and indulge in a few skirls or whatever it is Scots do when the sun goes doon.

In this paragraph Bill Bryson conveys his impression that the city is exciting and intriguing with details like:

- the station is at the heart of the city
- the main monuments are all floodlit
- the city is *abustle* with activity and people.

He suggests it is different by:

- referring to foods such as haggis and cock-a-leekie soup
- implying unfamiliarity with what Scots do after work.

Now make your own notes on the next three paragraphs and then use them to help you answer the question.

Question 1c) is asking you to select and collate information from *two* of the pieces in order to judge their effectiveness. You need to make notes on each of the areas listed in the question.

> c) All *three* pieces suggest that Edinburgh is a place worth visiting. Compare *two* of these, explaining which you found to be the most effective and why.
>
> You should comment on:
>   i what they are about
>   ii the way the information is presented
>   iii the way the writers use language
>   iv similarities and/or differences between the pieces
>   v your own response to the pieces.

i what they are about

You do not need to give a lot of detail for this. You should aim to summarize the content of each piece in a few sentences. Here are some points you might make about **Edinburgh**:

- it records the writer's impressions on arriving one evening by train
- he describes what he sees on his way to the Caledonian Hotel
- he explains how it felt like a 'different country'
- later he walks down the Royal Mile.

Now try to summarize the content of **Edinburgh, My Hometown** and **Edinburgh, So Much to See and Do**.

ii the way the information is presented

This section is more clearly relevant to **Edinburgh, My Hometown** and **Edinburgh, So Much to See and Do** than to **Edinburgh**.

Here are some notes on the presentational features in **Edinburgh, So Much to See and Do**:

- separate heading in larger print
- use of bold print to highlight the names of places to visit
- use of photograph as illustration of the Royal Botanic Garden
- separate boxed information on the Information Centre with address and telephone number.

Now make your own notes on **Edinburgh, My Hometown**.

When considering **Edinburgh** you could point out that, because of the type of writing it is, presentational features are not as relevant. You could then go on to comment simply on the way the ideas have been organized into paragraphs.

iii *the way the writers use language*

Here are some notes on the way the writer uses language in **Edinburgh, My Hometown**:

- written as a letter – directly addresses the audience, e.g. *No matter who you are, or what you like…*
- personal, informal style, e.g. *For the really sporty types I can highly recommend…*
- use of slang, e.g. *Edinburgh's got loads of theatres and cinemas…*
- relatively simple vocabulary and sentence structures, e.g. *It's full of interesting places and has lots of things to see and do.*

Now make your own notes on **Edinburgh, So Much to See and Do** and **Edinburgh**.

iv *similarities and/or differences between the pieces*

Some of these are quite obvious:

- they are all about the same city
- they mention some of the same places, e.g. Princes Street
- they all use language to highlight the charms of the city: *buzzing with life and excitement* (**Edinburgh, My Hometown**); *the perfect setting for a leisurely stroll* (**Edinburgh, So Much to See and Do**); *beautiful and beguiling city* (**Edinburgh**)
- they are written for different audiences
- **Edinburgh, My Hometown** and **Edinburgh** are written in the first person whereas **Edinburgh, So Much to See and Do** is written in the third person.

Can you think of any others?

v *your own response to the pieces*

When thinking about this you need to ask yourself questions like:

- did they communicate clearly and effectively?
- did they make me interested in the place?
- which one did I most enjoy reading? Why?

Now is the time to add any further comments you'd like to make on the pieces. For instance, you might want to comment on the humour in Bill Bryson's account or on the personal, matter-of-fact tone of the letter.

Now, draw all your ideas together and, remembering to concentrate on only *two* of the pieces, write out your answer to **1** c).

Exam Practice – Higher Tier

PAPER 1 SECTION A

- Read the visitor guide **Bedale – Gateway to the Dales**, the travel writing extract **The Yorkshire Dales** and the information on **Bedale** and **Malham**. Answer *all* parts of the question that follows.
- Spend *about one hour* on this section.

1 a)   i List *three* facts and *three* opinions from **Bedale – Gateway to the Dales**.

ii Write about the way the information in this piece is presented to the reader and comment on its effectiveness.

   b)   What reasons does the writer give in **The Yorkshire Dales** for finding the Dales *captivating beyond words*?

   c)   All three pieces relate to the same area of the country but were written for different audiences and purposes.

Which pieces made you feel a) most interested and b) least interested in the area? Explain why with reference to:
- content
- the language used
- the style of presentation
- the attitude to the reader
- your own response and preference.

BEDALE
GATEWAY TO THE DALES

Standing at the foot of the Dales, Bedale has been an important meeting point since Saxon times, when the track from Ripon joined the route from Northallerton to Wensleydale. The weekly market, granted its charter by Henry III in 1251, is still held on Tuesdays.

From these ancient beginnings, Bedale flourished as a thriving country town and has long been a favourite stopping off point for travellers on the Great North Road, now the A1. The many fine Georgian facades on the curving high street bear witness to the town's prosperity at the height of the coaching era, and the museum housed in the Palladian splendour of **Bedale Hall** has exhibits relating to local history and customs. A heritage trail leaflet gives an interesting introduction to the town's many historic buildings, which include an 18th century **Leech House** at Bedale Beck.

Today's travellers will find Bedale a convenient place to break a north-south journey. The town offers a range of accommodation, from charming bed and breakfast establishments to traditional coaching inns, and the shops stock quality local produce. Passing travellers may well find themselves seduced by the charms of the surrounding area, staying longer to explore the gently rolling countryside, where the River Ure finishes its descent through Wensleydale.

OTHER PLACES TO VISIT INCLUDE:

Thorp Perrow Arboretum
Snape. Tel: 01677 425323
Parkland housing over 1,000 species of trees in 85 acres, woodland walks, nature trails and tree trails.

Museum of Badges and Battledress
Crakehall. Tel: 01677 424444
An interesting collection of uniforms, badges and equipment used by the military from 1900 to the present day.

Marmion Tower
West Tanfield
14th Century gatehouse which was part of the former Tanfield Castle.

Crakehall Water Mill
Crakehall. Tel: 01677 423240
Fully restored watermill producing stoneground wholemeal flour in the traditional manner.

The Big Sheep and the Little Cow
Aiskew. Tel: 01677 422125
Small scale diary farm milking sheep and Dexter cows to produce cheese and ice cream.

VISITOR INFORMATION

MARKET DAY
Tuesday

TOURIST INFORMATION CENTRE ⓘ
Bedale Hall, Bedale. Tel: 01677 424604

BEDALE MUSEUM
Bedale. Tel: 01677 424604

BEDALE SWIMMING POOL
Firby Road, Bedale. Tel: 01609 779977
From May 1997 Tel: 01677 427272
Opening Summer 1997.

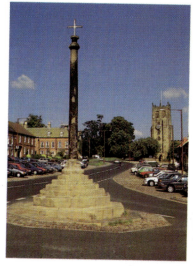

MARKET CROSS

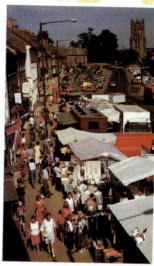

MARKET DAY

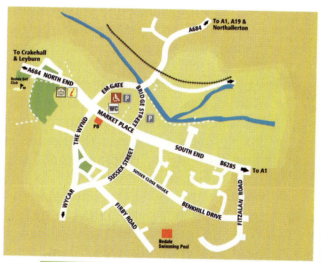

THE YORKSHIRE DALES

I suppose everybody has a piece of landscape somewhere that he finds captivating beyond words and mine is the Yorkshire Dales. I can't altogether account for it because you can easily find more dramatic landscapes elsewhere, even in Britain. All I can say is that the Dales seized me like a helpless infatuation when I first saw them and will not let me go. Partly, I suppose, it is the exhilarating contrast between the high fells, with their endless views, and the relative lushness of the valley floors, with their clustered villages and green farms. To drive almost anywhere in the Dales is to make a constant transition between these two hypnotic zones. It is wonderful beyond words. And partly it is the snug air of self-containment that the enclosing hills give, a sense that the rest of the world is far away and unnecessary, which is something you come to appreciate very much when you live there.

Every dale is a little world of its own to an extraordinary degree. I remember one sunny afternoon when we were new to our dale a car overturned in the road outside our gate with a frightful bang and a noise of scraping metal. The driver, it turned out, had clipped a grass bank and run up against a field wall, which had flipped the car onto its roof. I rushed out to find a local woman hanging upside down by her seatbelt, bleeding gently from a scalp wound and muttering dazed sentiments along the lines of having to get to the dentist and that this wouldn't do at all. While I was hopping around and making hyperventilating noises, two farmers arrived in a Land-Rover and climbed out. They gently hauled the lady from the car and sat her down on a rock. Then they righted the car and manoeuvred it out of the way. While one of them led the lady off to have a cup of tea and get her head seen to by his wife, the other scattered sawdust on an oil slick, directed traffic for a minute till the road was clear, then winked at me and climbed into his Land-Rover and drove off. The whole thing was over in less than five minutes and never involved the police or ambulance services or even a doctor. An hour or so later someone came along with a tractor and hauled the car away and it was as if it had never happened.

They do things differently in the Dales, you see. For one thing, people who know you come right in your house. Sometimes they knock once and shout 'Hullo!' before sticking their head in, but often they don't even do that. It's an unusual experience to be standing at the kitchen sink talking to yourself animatedly and then turning around to find a fresh pile of mail lying on the kitchen table. And I can't tell you the number of times I've had to dart into the pantry in my underpants at the sound of someone's approach and cowered breathless while they've shouted, 'Hullo! Hullo! Anyone t'home?' For a couple of minutes you can hear them clumping around in the kitchen, examining the messages on the fridge and holding the mail to the light. Then they come over to the pantry door and in a quiet voice they say, 'Just taking six eggs, Bill – all right?'

When we announced to friends and colleagues in London that we were moving to a village in Yorkshire, a surprising number made a sour face and said: 'Yorkshire? What, with Yorkshire people? How very ... interesting.' Or words to that effect.

I've never understood why Yorkshire people have this terrible reputation for being mean-spirited and uncharitable. I've always found them to be decent and open, and if you want to know your shortcomings, you won't find more helpful people anywhere. It's true that they don't exactly smother you with affection, which takes a little getting used to if you hail from a more gregarious part of the world, like anywhere else. Where I come from in the American Midwest if you move into a village or little town everybody comes to your house to welcome you like this is the happiest day in the history of the community – and everyone brings you a pie. You get apple pies and cherry pies and chocolate-cream pies. There are people in the Midwest who move house every six months just to get the pies.

In Yorkshire, that would never happen. But gradually, little by little, they find a corner for you in their hearts, and begin to acknowledge you when they drive past with what I call the Malhamdale wave. This is an exciting day in the life of any new arrival. To make the Malhamdale wave, pretend for a moment that you are grasping a steering wheel. Now very slowly extend the index finger of your right hand as if you were having a small involuntary spasm. That's it. It doesn't look like much, but it speaks volumes, believe me, and I shall miss it very much.

NOTES FROM A SMALL ISLAND BY BILL BRYSON

BEDALE AND MALHAM

BEDALE, *North Riding* (12-SE2688). The main street widens where the market is held then narrows at the top of the slope where the Church of St Gregory and Bedale Hall occupy opposite and commanding positions overlooking the agreeable townscape. The Church tower is 14th- and 15th-cent. work and has a porch on the south side. A room on the first floor was reached by a stair guarded by a portcullis, a defensive measure in case of Scottish raids. Walls in the nave may be Anglo-Saxon in origin; the east window was possibly brought from JERVAULX ABBEY. The alabaster effigy of Sir Brian Fitzalan who died in 1306 is one of the earliest of its kind. The rear of Bedale Hall is brick and matches the rest of the Georgian-style houses in the market place, but its front faces the country and is formal, in stone, dating from about 1730. It houses the Rural District Council office, a library and a museum. The great ballroom has a marvellous coved stucco ceiling with chubby figures fairly leaping over the cornice. The flying staircase has a bulb and umbrella balustrade. The house was built for Henry Peirse. This is splendid hunting country.

Snape Castle is 3 m. S., part ruin and part residence. The old chapel is preserved, a single room with Perpendicular windows and lively Dutch carvings of the life of Christ. Catherine Parr, sixth and last wife of Henry VIII, lived here.

MALHAM, *West Riding* (12-SD8963). The hamlet of stone cottages and a humped bridge is surrounded by moorland, high and wild, and some spectacular limestone scenery is within easy reach. Malham Cove is 3/4m. N., a curving sheer white cliff about 240 ft high of the Great Scar Limestone created by the Craven Fault. The River Aire steals out from its base. Above the rock stretches the dry valley along which, before the Ice Age, the Aire used to flow, plunging over the Cove in a great waterfall. It is a 2-m. walk up the valley to Malham Tarn (also accessible by road from Malham), a 150-acre natural lake formed by a dam of glacial moraine, on which there is skating in winter. Tarn House, the lake and 2,000 acres between Ribblesdale and Wharfedale now belong to the National Trust. The house is used by the Field Studies Council. It is said that Charles Kingsley, while staying at Tarn House, humorously explained the dark marks on the Cove as made by a chimney sweep falling over, and from this was born *The Water Babies*. Two m. NE. of Malham is **Gordale Scar**, also part of the CRAVEN Fault. It is possible to drive to within a quarter of a mile of this winding gorge with its splendid series of cascades.

Malham Cove

THE SHELL GUIDE TO ENGLAND EDITED BY JOHN HADFIELD

The examiner comments...

Question **1** a) part i asks you to:

> List *three* facts and *three* opinions in **Bedale – Gateway to the Dales**.

Here you are being tested on your ability to distinguish between fact and opinion and to select material according to purpose. In the information on Bedale fact and opinion are mixed together and it is up to you to separate them out.

Look at the first paragraph:

> Standing at the foot of the Dales, Bedale has been an important meeting point since Saxon times, when the track from Ripon joined the route from Northallerton to Wensleydale. The weekly market, granted its charter by Henry III in 1251, is still held on Tuesdays.

To say that Bedale stands at the foot of the Dales is obviously an opinion – who's to say where the foot of the Dales is? Also, while it may have been an important meeting point in Saxon times who can really say whether it is now. It is, however, factually correct to say that in Saxon times the track from Ripon joined the route from Northallerton to Wensleydale and that the weekly market, granted its charter by Henry III in 1251, is still held on Tuesdays.

Now read the second and third paragraphs closely and try to separate the facts from the opinions.

Part ii asks you to:

> Write about the way the information in **Bedale – Gateway to the Dales** is presented to the reader and comment on its effectiveness.

To do this you need to think about presentation and decide whether it has worked or not. Make your own notes on the following features:

- the heading and the sub-heading
- the range of type sizes and the use of bold print
- the use of photographs and a map
- the overall layout and clarity
- the different kinds of information given to the reader in different ways
- the final appeal to the reader to 'Come and Stay in Herriot Country'.

Now answer the question, remembering to comment clearly on the effectiveness of the various presentational features.

Question **1** b) asks you:

> What reasons does the writer give in **The Yorkshire Dales** for finding the Dales *captivating beyond words*?

Here you are being asked to follow his train of thought and identify the various points of his argument.

Look at the first paragraph in which he offers the following reasons:

- the contrast between the high fells and the valley floors
- the snug air of self-containment that the enclosing hills give
- the sense that the rest of the world is far away.

Put in your own words this might read:

He finds the contrast between the high fells and the valleys exhilarating, and likes the feeling of self-containment that the hills create and the sense of being separate from the rest of the world.

Now make your own notes on the other paragraphs and then answer the question, remembering to use your own words, rather than simply repeating those from the extract.

Question **1** c) points out that all three pieces relate to the same area of the country but were written for different audiences and purposes. You are asked:

> which pieces made you feel a) most interested and b) least interested in the area described. Explain why with reference to: content, language, presentation, attitude to the reader and your own response and preference.

To answer this question well you need to select and collate relevant information from *two* of the pieces and assess their overall effectiveness.

Here are some things you might say about **Bedale** and **Malham**.

Content: this is an informative guide to places of interest in the area and contains the most factual detail of the three pieces. We learn about the important geographical features and the relevant historical background. The text is scattered with a few personal opinions, e.g. *This is splendid hunting country*.

Language: the extracts are written in the third person and in standard English. The factual information is presented clearly and the writer uses a wide range of sentence structures from the simple *The house is used by the Field Studies Council* to the much more complex *The rear of Bedale Hall is brick and matches the rest of the Georgian-style houses in the market place, but its front faces the country and is formal, in stone, dating from about 1730.*

Adjectives are used freely throughout the text to help the reader visualize the place. In the first sentence of the extract on Malham we find the bridge being described as *humped*, the moorland as *high* and *wild* and the scenery as *spectacular*. In the same extract, verbs have been carefully selected to convey a particular idea to the reader. The River Aire *steals* out from its base and, before the Ice Age, used to *plunge* over the Cove.

Presentation: there aren't many presentational features here. Where appropriate, the text is divided into paragraphs. Places of interest are sometimes in capital letters and some other place names, but not all, are highlighted in bold print. The photograph, in black and white, gives a clear visual image of the dramatic scenery to be found at Malham.

Attitude to reader: the writer assumes that the reader will have an interest in particular topics and focuses on these, e.g. historical detail. The extracts are written in the third person and the reader is not addressed directly.

Personal response: obviously this is up to you to decide. When giving your personal response you should aim to give a balanced answer, pointing out the positive and negative aspects of the text and explaining why you do or do not find it appealing. Your opening sentence might be:

This would be of particular use and interest to me if I was visiting the area though it is not something I would normally choose to read.

You would follow this with a clear explanation of why.

Now make notes on **Bedale – Gateway to the Dales** and **The Yorkshire Dales** before answering the question.

Section B:
Writing to Argue, Persuade or Instruct

In your exam you will be given a choice of writing tasks which require you to argue, persuade or instruct. These tasks will be linked to the topics or the themes of the non-fiction materials in Section A of the paper.

Your examiner will be looking for a range of writing skills. Some of these relate to the basic mechanics of writing, without which the reader may become unsure of your meaning.

- Your handwriting should be legible and the presentation of your work should be neat and clear.

- Words should be spelt correctly.

- Your writing should be correctly punctuated.

- You are expected to organize your ideas in sentences and paragraphs and to communicate them clearly.

Other skills are perhaps less obvious and relate to the effectiveness of your writing.

- Your vocabulary should be varied and appropriate, demonstrating a knowledge and understanding of a range of words.

- Your sentences should be correctly structured and varied.

- You should show an awareness of both audience and purpose and the ability to adapt your writing style to suit these.

In this section we look at the types of writing you will be asked to produce in the exam, and the ways in which you can use and improve the skills you already have, as well as developing new skills. There are lots of examples of different kinds of writing for you to look at and assess for their effectiveness.

Writing for audience and purpose

Audience

The audience of a piece of writing is the intended reader, the person (or people) you are writing for.

ACTIVITY 1

Read the extracts below and then answer these questions:

- Where do you think they come from?

- Who do you think they are aimed at? Consider age, gender and interests.

- How do words such as *hot*, *high-maintenance girl* and *fab* help you to identify the audience in extract A?

- What is unusual about the use of language in extract B?

- How does the appearance of each text help you to identify the audience?

A ▼

hot summer cuts

ARE YOU A HIGH- MAINTENANCE GIRL? OR DO YOU HAVE JUST FIVE MINUTES IN THE MORNING TO **MAKE YOURSELF LOOK FAB?** WE GUARANTEE THAT EVEN THE LAZIEST OF YOU WILL FIND A HAIRDO YOU CAN PERFECT AMONG THIS LOT!

**FACE SHAPE:
SQUARE, LONG OR OVAL**
Divide hair into large sections. Apply thickening spray to the roots of each section and blow-dry. Use a touch of wax to define wispy ends.

**FACE SHAPE:
OVAL, HEART
OR LONG**
Finger-dry hair until almost dry, spray on a serum and blow-dry. Part and smooth one side down with serum.

**FACE SHAPE:
SQUARE, LONG OR OVAL**
Section off hair, apply firm-hold styling spray to the roots and blow-dry. Smooth with serum.

B ▼

FOLLOW ALL THE HOTTEST ACTION IN THE SPORTED! GUIDE TO SUMMER

'HAPPY DAYS ARE HERE AGAIN, THE SUN IS IN the sky'. Summer's fast approaching and the temperature's rising here at SPORTED! Towers. There's nothing that SPORTED! likes more than top, flash-as-yer-like sporting action on a hot, sun-baked day. And if you're the same as us you've got one helluva summer in store coz everything's going down in '97!

. SUGAR

SPORTED

ACTIVITY 2

- Read the extract below and those on page 60 and try to work out who they were written for.

- What features of the writing and its appearance helped you to identify the intended audience? Give specific examples.

Long ago, people thought that the sky was a dome filled with stars, hanging over the earth.

After Galileo made the first telescope it was easier to observe the sky and have a clearer idea of the stars and planets.

We now know that our Solar System is only a tiny part of the whole universe.

Our Solar System is made up of the planets, including Earth, and the star we call the Sun, and, with 400 billion other stars, is part of a great galaxy.

A ◀

MY PICTURE WORD BOOK OF PEOPLE, PLACES AND THINGS

reviews

SURFING ON THE WAVES OF A STRANGE SEA

CD ROM: THE UNEXPLAINED

FLAGTOWER (www.flagtower.com). 1996, RRP £29.99. HOTLINES: UK 0500 486 500, USA 1-800-338-2006. MINIMUM CONFIGURATION: 486DX-66 CPU, 8 MB RAM, 2XCD, 256 COLOUR VIDEO, WINDOWS 3.1, MOUSE, 16-BIT SOUNDCARD.

FORTEAN TIMES

The so-called 'paranormal' is an ideal field for encyclopaedic projects and this CD-ROM – nothing to do with the seminal partwork of the same title from Orbis in the 1980s – makes a bold attempt but, sad to say, misses the target. Its aims were ambitious but thwarted by the disproportionate assignment of resources to presentation at the expense of depth of research.

Six main headings – 'Strange Phenomena', 'UFOs and Ufology' 'Mysterious Beings' 'Ghosts and Spirits' 'Earth Mysteries' and 'Beyond Science' – are each divided into five or six topics, each with a supporting array of sub-topics and pictures.

B ▲

To Newcastle-upon-Tyne
October 2nd

This morning we drove down to the quayside under the green struts of the High Level Bridge. All the people who had been at the shopping precinct had now come down to the river to spend. Such big babies being pushed in prams, all eating chips from little cardboard trays. The traders were selling much of the same sort of essential goods as anywhere else, nylon tiger-skin rugs, fur snakes as draught stoppers; there was a pet stall littered with puppies rolling in sawdust and diarrhoea, and birds in cages, and rats. 'Take one home,' urged the stall-holder. 'Give the mother-in-law a treat!'

… Going to my [hotel] I keep passing bearded gentlemen who roll rather than walk. I've been told they're Norwegian sea-captains.

From my window I have a view of the cemetery of St John the Baptist Church, and only a small slice of motorway. Went to sleep last night to the sound of bagpipes.

C ▲

BY BERYL BAINBRIDGE

Purpose

The purpose of a piece of writing is the reason for which it has been written. It may have been written to explain, entertain, inform, express feelings, persuade or organize ideas. These are just a few of the possibilities and a writer may well have more than one purpose in mind.

Look at this example and then answer the questions below.

ACTIVITY 3

- Which of these words best describe the purpose of this item?

  inform   explain   entertain   persuade   express feelings

- How do words such as *get going for*, *help* and *do it for* reflect the purpose?

- How does the appearance of the text help to reinforce its purpose? Think about:

  the drawing   the layout   the variations in print size.

ACTIVITY 4

- Look at the text below and the text on page 63 and try to work out why they were written.

- What is it about the way they are written that gives you clues as to their purpose?

  Sometimes you need to make very clear comments on the way words are being used in order to achieve a particular purpose.

- Look again at the leaflet, **Throwing light on Sunrays**. What is the precise effect of words such as:

  leathery   *wrinkled prematurely*

  ageing   *dangerous*?

  How do these words reinforce the message of the leaflet?

- Now look again at the letter, **European friends**. What is the tone of the letter (e.g. angry, friendly, humorous) and how is it achieved through the words and phrases the writer uses?

European friends

I am currently living in Germany, working with disabled children. I am writing to say that the highlight of my week is when my mum sends me a copy of *The Big Issue*. I find the magazine brilliant and a very good read. The bloke my mum buys it from is called Paul and sells *The Big Issue* outside Boots, Huddersfield. I would like to say keep up the good work, even though it's hard. And now you know that *The Big Issue* is read by a couple of people who live in another country.

Zo Last, Germany

THE BIG ISSUE

THROWING *light* ON SUNRAYS

Sunlight contains bands of ultra-violet radiation, or UV for short. Scientists believe that two of these bands, UVA and UVB, can damage our skin in slightly different ways.

UVA – this penetrates deep into the skin and can cause it to become leathery and wrinkled prematurely.

UVB – this is absorbed in the upper layers of the skin and stimulates production of melanin, the dark pigment which forms your tan. UVB is the main cause of sunburn and is thought to be responsible for most skin cancers.

Remember the difference by thinking of
UVA for **Ageing**   and   **UVB** for **Burning**.

Which sunscreen?

Sunscreens can block both UVA and UVB. But the SPF number tells you only how well a sunscreen blocks UVB. It's harder to measure its ability to block UVA. Different companies may use different ways of measuring this. As UVB is more dangerous than UVA, you'd be wise to choose a sunscreen according to its SPF rating.

The ozone layer

Only a little UVB finds it way to the earth's surface – most of it is absorbed in the atmosphere and by the ozone layer. It is possible that in the future ozone depletion could lead to more UVB reaching us. The Government constantly monitors levels of UVB in Britain and there is no sign of long-term increase yet.

What about sunbeds ?

Sunbeds emit UVA and some UVB so excessive use may lead to skin cancer. If you burn easily or if you have had skin cancer you are advised not to use them. Children under 16 should not use sunbeds. In any case, a sunbed tan gives you little protection against sunburn.

Feel good, feel safe

The warmth of the sun can make us feel happy, healthy, relaxed and alive. Enjoy these good feelings without the ill-effects of over-exposure. Simply follow the advice in this leaflet.

7

ACTIVITY 5

Jot down a list of all the different things you have written in the last two days and try to identify the audience and purpose(s) of each of them.

e.g. notes on volcanoes in Geography

audience: self and teacher

purpose: to select important details and for revision at a later date.

Holiday brochures

Holiday brochures have two main purposes. First, they are designed to interest the reader and make him/her want to go to a particular place, and secondly they aim to persuade the reader to choose that holiday above all others. Obviously, different kinds of holidays are geared to different kinds of people.

ACTIVITY 6

1 **On the following pages you will find two extracts from holiday brochures. Match the following statements to the appropriate extract:**

- This holiday would appeal to people interested in history.
- Families would enjoy this holiday.
- Children are welcome but must be supervised at all times.
- Onsite entertainment is offered at the hotel.
- This is for people who want to get away from it all.
- This holiday is not suitable for disabled people.
- The nightlife is lively.
- This is for people who like their time to be organized for them.
- Children probably wouldn't enjoy this holiday.
- People who like peace and quiet should come here.

2 **Write a short description of the kind of people you think would be interested in these holidays.**

3 **Explain clearly how each brochure targets audience and purpose.**

Holiday brochures seek to persuade, and in doing so they often use language to create a particular picture in the mind of the reader.

ACTIVITY 7

1 **Here is a selection of words and phrases taken from the two holiday brochures. Find them in the extracts and, for each one, explain how language is being used to persuade the reader:**

our escape	*amazing archaeological find*
visitors flock here in their droves	*a haven for sailors*
Orcadian adventure	*captures the perfect holiday mood*
indulge yourself	*a glittering line-up*
star-studded live cabaret	*the glorious rolling Sussex Downs*
the Regency splendours of Brighton	*it's a lot closer than you think*
meet new friends	

2 **Write a description of your classroom along the lines of the descriptions in the brochures. Persuade your reader that it is a wonderful place to be!**

OCEAN HOTEL
BRIGHTON
SALTDEAN

AROUND & ABOUT

The Ocean Hotel overlooks the sea from the hill at Saltdean, and is on the edge of the glorious rolling Sussex Downs, only 5 miles from the Regency splendours of Brighton, the Royal Pavilion and Palace Pier.

HOTEL ENTERTAINMENT

- Top Live Cabaret • Ballroom, Disco & Modern Sequence Dancing
- Late Night Sing-a-Long Karaoke Bar
- Bingo • Amusements • Children's Funclub

HOTEL FACILITIES

- Indoor Heated Pool • Hairdressing Salon*
- Sauna* & Sunbeds* • Green Baize Snooker Club • Darts • Snooker
- Indoor Bowls • Children's Playground
- Landscaped Gardens with Putting Green
- Mini Market • Newsagents & Gift Shop
- Boutique • Photo Developing Service*
- Lifts To Most Floors • Car Park & On Street Parking

*Available for an additional fee

A regular Bus service runs from opposite the Hotel into Brighton Town Centre.

Please note that the Ocean Hotel has certain venues whose access may cause difficulties to disabled customers.

FOOD & DRINK

- Dining Room & Premier Dining Area
- Porthole Bistro • Ocean Ballroom Bar
- The P.O.S.H. Bar

FACILITIES FOR CHILDREN

CHILDREN aged 2 to 14 years are half the adult price on all breaks (except in Premier accommodation). Infants under 2 go Free (when sharing their parents room).

Please note that children are welcome and the Children's Funclub is open at limited times (as advertised at the Entertainments Desk). We regret that this is not a directly supervised child-minding service. Parents are therefore asked to note that children must be supervised at all times.

There's something special about the Southcoast and the Ocean Hotel at Saltdean, near Brighton that certainly captures the perfect holiday mood.

Magnificent views and a warm, friendly atmosphere create a relaxing and action-packed experience for all the family. Kids will have a really exciting time in the Children's Funclub and everyone can enjoy a splash in the heated indoor funpool. Indulge yourself, laze in the sauna, drop into the boutique or have your hair styled in our salon. Pot the black on the snooker tables, or join in a game of darts or bingo – you set the pace and do exactly as you feel.

Meet new friends over a cool drink in the 'P.O.S.H' Bar or enjoy a leisurely meal at the new 'Porthole' Bistro. Choose your partner and take your pick of ballroom, modern and disco styles in the 'Ocean' Ballroom.

As night falls, a glittering line-up of entertainment unfolds with star-studded live cabaret and plenty of sing-a-long and karaoke fun. You may even find time to explore the local sights, including France - it's a lot closer than you think!

CHILDREN GO FREE ON SELECTED DATES SEE PAGE 67 FOR DETAILS

Orcadian Adventure
"In The Wake Of The Vikings"

Skara Brae, Orkney

Ring of Brodgar

Below: Churchill's Barriers

7 DAYS SCENIC CENTRED HOLIDAY

First Day, Sunday: We make our escape to Orkney, a unique island with welcoming people whose relaxed way of life is alive with legends from the Viking era. Our journey north brings us to Aviemore where we stay overnight at the Stakis Badenoch Hotel.

Second Day, Monday: We continue north through Helmsdale, Wick and John O' Groats to Thurso to board the ferry at Scrabster. We then sail to Stromness for four nights at the Stromness Hotel.

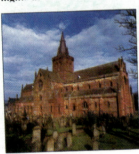
Kirkwall

Third Day, Tuesday: A full day tour of Orkney's West Mainland, stopping at Skara Brae, on the lovely Bay of Skaill. Man lived here in Neolithic times in a village which was later preserved by a sandstorm. Today this amazing archaeological find is one of Scotland's top attractions and visitors flock here in their droves. We circle the coast to Kirkwall and return to Stromness with views of the large prehistoric tomb of Maes Howe.

Fourth Day, Wednesday: A full day excursion to Kirkwall on the narrow strait that separates east and west mainlands overlooking Scapa Bay, and to South Ronaldsay. Kirkwall dates back over 800 years to the times of the Norse Earl Rognvald who built St. Magnus Cathedral using local red and yellow sandstone.

Fifth Day, Thursday: We spend a day at leisure in Stromness which has been a haven for sailors since Viking times. Walk the town's narrow streets and get the feeling of being in another century - until you walk into the modern Pier Arts Centre.

Sixth Day, Friday: Take a last look at Orkney as we leave on the ferry to Scrabster and travel south via Wick, Helmsdale and Inverness into the Spey Valley to stay overnight at the Stakis Badenoch Hotel, Aviemore.

Seventh Day, Saturday: We leave Aviemore and travel home from our Orcadian adventure.

DATES & PRICES		HOLIDAY No. 1326Y
May	18	£ 325
Jun	1	£ 345
Jun	15	£ 345
Jun	29	£ 345
Jul	13	£ 345
Jul	27	£ 345
Aug	10	£ 345
Aug	24	£ 345
Sep	7	£ 345

- Departs **Sunday** Returns **Saturday**
- Departure Code **A**
- See pages **127** to **129** for departure details
- **6 Nights** Dinner, bed & breakfast
- All rooms with private facilities
- Free included excursions
- No single supplements

NEW FOR 1997 - TOTAL LUGGAGE HANDLING SERVICE

YOUR HOLIDAY HOTEL

STROMNESS HOTEL - Stromness, Orkney. Tel. 01856 850298 ♕♕♕

In a central situation in the quiet fishing port of Stromness, overlooking the harbour and Scapa Flow. • All bedrooms have private facilities, telephone, television and tea/coffee making equipment • Lift to all floors • Residents' cocktail bar for that pre-dinner drink
• The Hamnavoe lounge bar with panoramic views
• Three course evening dinner plus tea or coffee.

Stromness

ACTIVITY 8

Now read this extract from a very different holiday brochure and comment on the following:

- its intended audience
- the interests the audience is expected to have
- the type of language being used and the reason for this
- its overall effectiveness.

Summer '97

THE GIGS – THE INFO

Take only the best ideas
add food, drink, entertainment, reps, you, your mates, a load of same vibe others – and they've been **Clubbed!!!!!!**

The Best Ideas
Greek night, Cruise, Party Night, Rave Night, Reggae Night, Waterpark, Cabaret

Clubbed!!!!
Go Greek, A life on The Ocean Wave, Stag 'N Hen, Surprise Special, Caribbean Night, Watercity, Live!

The Biggest of the Greek islands. Way down South. Deep blue seas. Banana plantation. Hot days and hotter nights. And a little place called Malia.

Malia the old village nestling on a hill about a mile from the beach. Malia the beach, a stonking stretch of golden sand. In between The Strip. Bursting with bars. Rammed with restaurants. Chocker with clubs. End to end with entertainment.

So that's you sorted. Start one end at the beginning of the week and see you in a fortnight. We added up the party places and stopped counting at 100, and still had some to go. Bet you don't even make it halfway. Don't miss Zoo Club though. Or the Electra Crazy Bar.

Meanwhile down on the waterfront, cats are chillin in the sun. Or snoozin round the pool. And grabbin a beer and a bite in the taverna. Refuel, recharge those batteries, and don't overdo it on the first day. Burn out alert! If you can't stand the heat head for the old village and cool off under a shady grapevine with a beer or three.

Of course if you're into history you'll know the ancient Romans used to come here for their hols. Do us a favour though – leave the anorak at home.

ACTIVITY 9

Imagine you work for a holiday company and have been asked to write inserts for a number of different brochures on the following subjects. You will need to be creative and write about the things most likely to appeal to your targeted audience. There are some clues in brackets. Remember to make your tone appropriate to your audience. Underline any words or phrases you use which you think are particularly persuasive.

- The swimming pool in a hotel suitable for families (exciting, adventurous, clean, safe, warm).
- The quiet country surroundings of a cottage intended for the over-sixties (peaceful, good for walking but not hilly, attractive, natural).
- The range of night-time activities for teenagers in a holiday resort (lively, exciting, late, varied, friendly, trouble-free).

Writing for a younger audience

You might be asked to write for a younger audience. If so, there are certain things you need to be aware of.

1 Very young children have a limited vocabulary so words should be as simple as possible.

2 They have difficulty in handling lots of different ideas at the same time so sentences should be short, simply structured and contain one central idea.

3 Ideas in separate sentences should be closely linked so that the child can follow the points that are being made.

ACTIVITY 10

How does the writer meet the needs of young children in the following extract from a book which deals with the subject of *Being Born and Growing Up*? Focus on the words used, sentence structure and length and the linking of ideas.

BEING BORN and GROWING UP

apple pip   poppy seed

Everything that a plant needs to help it to develop is contained within its seed. Look at the apple and the poppy seeds.

Protected by the earth the seeds develop shoots which grow towards the light. Seedlings appear.

The poppy only grows for a single season. The apple tree keeps on growing year after year.

The hen is keeping her eggs warm. Inside each egg a chick develops.

When the chicks are fully formed, they use their little beaks to break open the eggshells.

Some of the newly-hatched chicks will grow up to be cockerels and some will grow into hens.

After a month the chicks have grown crests on their heads. It is still hard to tell male from female.

Now the chicks have grown up to become a cockerel and a hen. Soon some eggs will be laid, and more chicks will be hatched.

The puppies are sucking milk from the mother dog's teats. Puppies develop and grow very quickly.

At four months a puppy is independent, playful and curious. When he grows up, he will get together with a female, called a bitch, and more puppies will be born.

development: is the transformation of everything which grows.

Sow some seeds and watch the plants grow. There are suggestions on page 61.

MY PICTURE WORD BOOK OF PEOPLE, PLACES AND THINGS

Writing for older children

Older children, say in the nine to twelve age group, have a much broader understanding of words and can grasp the meaning of quite complex sentences. Even so, they are not likely to be interested in material written for an older or adult audience. You have to work particularly hard to capture their imaginations and make them read on. Here is the introduction to a history book with a difference:

History with the nasty bits left in!

Cruel Kings and Mean Queens gives you the horrible historical facts on all our shocking sovereigns, from William the Conker right up to Lizzie the Last. It'll tell you what you really want to know, like …

- which king died after falling off the toilet
- why people thought King John was a werewolf
- why Queen Anne's feet were covered in garlic

… and much more, including foul but fascinating facts on horrible habits, ghastly palace ghosts, and the dreadful royal doctors of days gone by. This grippingly gruesome guide lets you into the secrets of our mad, menacing and murderous monarchs and the terrible times in which they ruled.

HISTORY HAS NEVER BEEN SO HORRIBLE!

CRUEL KINGS AND MEAN QUEENS BY TERRY DEARY

Look at and think about:

- the use of exclamation marks and bullet points
- puns on names, e.g. William the Conker
- frequent use of alliteration, e.g. *horrible habits*; *grippingly gruesome guide*; *mad, menacing and murderous monarchs.*

ACTIVITY 11

Write short introductions to two books – one for seven-year-olds and one for eleven-year-olds. Both books are called **Your TV Guide** and are about television. The idea is to give children more information on their favourite programmes and how they are made. Your introduction could include:

- questions children might want answered
- comments on the importance of television today
- details of particular programmes.

Remember to make your introductions appropriate to your audience and purpose. They should be lively and interesting.

POINTS *to remember*

- The audience of a piece of writing is the intended reader.
- The purpose of a piece of writing is the reason for which it has been written.
- Language can be used to persuade the reader to a particular point of view.
- Language, sentence structure and tone should be adapted to suit audience and purpose.
- It is very important both for your own writing and for your understanding of what you read that you develop your awareness of audience and purpose.

Writing reports and articles

Reports

A report tells the story of something that has happened. Reports most commonly appear in newspapers in which journalists inform their readers of recent local, national and international events.

Newspaper stories tend to follow a similar pattern. The first paragraph usually contains the main points of the story and aims to grab the reader's attention. People tend to read newspapers quickly and often decide whether or not to continue reading on the basis of the first paragraph. The subsequent paragraphs provide further information and usually answer the questions: Who? What? Where? When? Why? How?

ACTIVITY 1

Read the reports on page 72. For each report try to find the answers to the following questions: Who? What? Where? When? Why? How?

Reports tend to be written in the past tense. When writing a report you often need to refer to what certain people have said. This might be done through direct speech: *'It happened outside my pub,' said landlady Mandy Ward of the Bay Horse*, or through indirect speech: *All French teams are now involved in doping, Delion claimed.*

ACTIVITY 2

Write a report for a local newspaper about an imagined or real street incident. It could involve:

- a fight
- an accident
- shoplifting
- a lost child
- traffic lights failure
- a parade.

Remember to include the important details in your first paragraph and then to develop them further in the rest of your report. Aim to include at least one eye-witness account.

Jilted lover wrapped up like a "mummy"

A JILTED lover ended up being wrapped like a "mummy" when tourists stepped in to prevent him causing further mayhem in Masham Market Place.

Christopher Palfrey had just driven 150 miles to the market town when tourists, including an Australian couple, saw him hanging on the door of a car with a young woman desperately trying to escape his clutches.

Eyewitnesses said 33-year-old Palfrey crashed his van into a wall and was then seen hanging on to the outside passenger door of his former girlfriend's car as she drove round the Market Square before smashing into another vehicle.

As she tried to run away from him, community spirited shop staff, businessmen and visitors alerted the police to the mayhem before stepping in to take action.

"It happened outside my pub," said landlady Mandy Ward of the Bay Horse. "There was a terrific thud and apparently all hell was let loose. An Australian couple then helped to arrest the man trying to get into the woman's car. Fortunately there were road works nearby and it appears everyone rallied round," she said.

"I understand they dragged the man to the ground and tied him up using the red and white plastic tape surrounding the road works to bind him like a mummy."

Palfrey was eventually dumped in the road and, while one person sat on him, others directed the traffic round him until the police arrived.

On Wednesday, Palfrey, of The Avenue, Acocks Green, Birmingham, pleaded guilty at Northallerton Magistrates' Court to charges arising from the incident last August, including using threatening behaviour.

He also admitted being a disqualified driver and driving with excess alcohol and without insurance.

Charges of assaulting Australian holidaymakers Joanne and Ian Sherwin were not proceeded with after prosecutor Jane Cook said they had now returned home. Palfrey, who also pleaded guilty to further offences committed in Birmingham, was remanded on bail for the preparation of probation and medical reports. Magistrates ordered that he must not visit North Yorkshire until his next court appearance.

NORTHALLERTON, THIRSK AND BEDALE TIMES

Riders claim doping rife at the top

DOPING has become commonplace among professional riders in recent years, involving most of the sport's top 50, according to two recently retired riders.

Gilles Delion, who stopped riding at the end of last season, said in an article in the French sports daily L'Equipe that a French team director told him that "you couldn't be among the world's best 50 riders if you didn't take EPO, and it's been that way for quite a while."

EPO (erythropoietin) is a performance-enhancing substance that stimulates the production of red blood cells which transport oxygen around the body. All French teams are now involved in doping, Delion claimed.

Delion, regarded as a highly promising rider who never quite reached the very top, despite winning the Tour of Lombardy in 1990 and a stage of the 1992 Tour de France, said he saw riders looking for ice cubes in hotels to keep the vials containing EPO cool.

"I also saw a rider take EPO," he said. "I wasn't shocked because I knew such things happened but usually the riders would lock themselves up in the bathroom."

Nicolas Aubier, who retired at the end of last season because he felt the sport had been debased by doping, said he was forced to use prohibited substances. "Frankly I can't imagine a rider belonging to the top 100 and not taking EPO, growth hormones or another product," he told L'Equipe. "The problem is that the use of doping products has become so general that anybody not taking anything is regarded as abnormal."

THE GUARDIAN

More about reports

You might also find reports in a company's or charity's information pack. These tend to be written more formally, outlining the factual details clearly and precisely. The following extract appeared in an ACTIONAID Community Report:

> IN THIS REPORT we would like to introduce you to one of the basic needs of people in Bangladesh, improved access to good water and sanitation conditions, and how ACTIONAID is trying to overcome this situation in the Jamalpur project area.
>
> In poor countries millions of people die every year because of polluted water and poor sanitation. Bangladesh in this regard is not different. The situation is even worse in rural areas, especially in the remotest corners where people need to walk for about two to three kilometres to collect a bucket of safe drinking water.
>
> Water and Sanitation projects have received a higher priority in our project here and are now an integral part of ACTIONAID'S development approach. The objective is to ensure availability and secure future management of adequate and safe drinking water and to improve sanitary practices, aiming to achieve the goal of 'Health for all by the year 2000'.

Note that this report, like the newspaper reports, summarizes the main details in the opening paragraph. Unlike the newspaper reports it is written in the present tense.

ACTIVITY 3

Many schools now produce a Governors' Report which is sent to parents annually to inform them of the school's activities and achievements. This tends to be a mixture of formal reporting on exam results, for example, and more informal accounts of highlights of the school's year.

Write a report for parents about a recent important event that has taken place in your school. This might be a school trip, a sporting achievement, a school play or concert, or something similar.

Articles

An article may share several features in common with a report. For example, an article may also provide specific details about something that has happened. A piece of writing in a magazine or newspaper may be referred to as an article by one person and a report by another. Generally speaking, though, an article is more narrative in approach and may be more heavily dependent on the development of an argument. You will find articles in newspapers and magazines covering an enormous range of subjects from love and 'choosing the right partner', to an analysis of 'How to get the best out of your mountain bike!'

ACTIVITY 4

Read the extracts from two very different kinds of articles on pages 75 and 76.

Compare the two extracts by looking at:

- what they are about

- how the ideas are organized

- how they are presented – do they use sub-headings, captions, pictures?

- the style in which they are written – what sort of vocabulary do they use? How long are the sentences? How long are the paragraphs?

- the tone (is it humorous, serious, angry, concerned, neutral?)

- the attitude to the reader (is it patronizing? Does it expect the reader to know a lot?)

Clearly there is enormous flexibility in how you write an article. Your style will be partly determined by your purpose and audience but you still have a lot of freedom in how you deliver your information and point of view.

ACTIVITY 5

Write the opening three paragraphs for articles on two of the subjects listed below. Try to use a different style of writing and tone for each subject.

- The importance of presents at Christmas

- An interview with a famous person

- Winning the lottery

- Banning the sale of cigarettes.

POINTS *to remember*

- The first paragraph of a newspaper story often contains the main points.
- An article is generally more narrative in approach than a report.
- When writing an article or a report, content, style and tone will be determined by purpose and audience.

THE GOOD SLEEP GUIDE

There's no need to put up with sleepless nights, or interrupted sleep patterns. Dr Thomas Stuttaford, Medical Correspondent for *The Times*, reports

Insomnia is an important problem and one which deserves to be taken seriously by the sufferers and their doctors. Yet over a third of patients who are regularly troubled by sleeplessness never consult their GP. Young people, in particular, fail to mention insomnia when they visit the surgery although it may be an important symptom of deep-seated troubles.

Even the most amenable person may shout after a few nights of disturbed sleep, for as a recent survey has shown, 75 per cent of patients who have had a bad night find that the next day they are moody and depressed. Young people are less irritable after a sleepless night than those who are older.

However crotchety, only a small fraction, about 10 per cent, of over-65s find that sleeplessness affects their concentration the next day, possibly because by then many are retired and life is less demanding.

Conversely, over 40 per cent of the under-45s think that poor sleep is detrimental to their work and concentration and has had an adverse effect on their career prospects. One in ten drivers involved in a road accident blame it on a poor night's sleep. There is evidence that actually falling asleep at the wheel causes more traffic accidents than too much alcohol.

A third of all poor sleepers blame insomnia for a lack of domestic harmony. These are usually younger patients. Some find that it leads to shouting matches with their spouse or children. Other people claim that when they are tired they are unable to take an interest in family activities. Loss of sexual drive is a constant complaint, and most say they are grumpy, uncommunicative and lacklustre.

It is not only the family who suffer; patients who sleep badly tend to neglect their friends and their social life shrinks. Over 90 per cent of sufferers claim it adversely affects their life in some way the following day.

WHAT SORT OF INSOMNIAC ARE YOU?

There are different patterns of insomnia and doctors will question patients carefully to find out which type they have. Some find it hard to get off to sleep. This tends to be associated with excessive anxiety. Others wake in the night or in the early hours of the morning and then find it hard to go back to sleep; often they succeed just when it's time to get up. This pattern is found in depressed patients. Finally, others appear to have had a full night's sleep but wake tired. These people may have a sleep rhythm that is disturbed by abnormal snoring.

Insomnia can also be secondary to other medical conditions, with arthritis being the most common. Arthritic pains, together with reduced daytime activities and exercise are among the reasons why older people are more likely to suffer sleeplessness. Women are four times as likely as men to see their doctor about insomnia.

WHAT YOU NEVER KNEW ABOUT SLEEP

● More than 10 hours and less than 6, is associated with increased mortality.

● 30 per cent of the population think they are insomniacs.

● Even people who claim to have had an entirely wakeful night usually have some sleep.

● There are different types of insomnia caused by different conditions. Some people suffer from more than one type of disturbed sleep pattern.

● The average time taken to fall asleep is 15 minutes. Normal sleep is divided into four stages. In each stage, the level of unconsciousness becomes progressively deeper; when waking the pattern is reversed. The cycle is repeated four or five times a night.

● Dreaming usually starts about an hour after falling asleep. A sleeper deprived of dream time wakes up cross and irritable.

● 10 per cent of sufferers blame poor sleep as the cause of a road accident.

THE BELLS, THE BELLS!

ROGER ST PIERRE gives audible warning of new ideas for canalside cyclists

Ting-a-ling-a-ling! Time was when it was deemed obligatory to have a bell on your bike. That was before, somewhere in the Fifties and after a long fight, the cycling lobby managed to win their argument that a shouted warning of "Oi! Get out of the way!" qualified as the Road Traffic Act's requisite 'audible warning of approach'.

Though manufacturers continued to supply a bell with each new bike they sold – somewhere separately in the cardboard bike box and usually destined to be thrown out with the wrappings – to all intents bicycle bells went the way of cycle clips.

The arguments had been cogent: that the human voice carries further than any bicycle bell – though not as far as an electrically powered air horn! – and that, in any event, fingers grabbing for the bell would be better used grabbing for the brakes.

End of story ... or so we thought. Now, however, well over three decades later there are people who would like cycle bell manufacturers to get back into business (I hope they'll produce those natty little numbers in glitzy anodised finishes rather than drab aluminium or plain chrome!).

It seems that walkers, anglers and everyman and his dog wants bikies to (a) be more considerate (fair enough) and (b) to unfailingly give warning of imminent approach (though I guess, before too long they'll be complaining just as stridently about being disturbed by all the resultant noise).

It seems that the British Waterways Board is looking at the possibility of charging – yes, charging – cyclists for the use of their towpaths. It's only an idea up for discussion and don't blame them for looking into it; Government pressure is now for all public bodies to maximise their income potential rather than being fully supported out of general taxation as was the case in the days when public service was regarded as a mission from God and not a dirty word.

The argument is that canalboaters pay to glide along the waters and anglers pay to fish in them, so why shouldn't cyclists pay for the right to ride alongside them, especially since it is the board which has to upkeep the tracks. We cyclists might say that, in that case, surely pedestrians should be made to pay as well – especially since there are far more of them than there are of us.

The immediate riposte to that is that charging pedestrians would not be practical – how would you collect? Which brings us back to those bells, for one idea being put forward is that rather than carrying a permit in our wallets or a licence disc on our bikes we should be issued with a bell to be fitted to our bikes for the double purpose of proving we've paid and satisfying the demand from other canal users for us to give better warning of our approach.

Nobody has thought through what will happen if other authorities pursue the idea – will our bikes end up bedecked with a variety of bells and horns, each with their own distinctive tone, and what sanction will be applied if you accidentally use the wrong one? Outrageous? Maybe, but it is a problem of our own making because while there are lots of complaints about inconsiderate cyclists it seems there are very few against pedestrians, except, that is, dog-walkers, who allow their animals to foul the canalpaths – and there is talk of making them take out a licence too.

> The arguments had been cogent: that the human voice carries further than any bicycle bell – though not as far as an electrically powered air horn!

Writing letters

There are many times when you might need, or want, to write a letter.
Here are just a few possibilities:

- to apply for a job or a place on a course
- to request and/or give information
- to keep in touch with family or friends
- to express a particular point of view.
- to complain or praise

Letter-writing can be divided into two main categories: formal and informal.

Formal letter-writing

There are many different ways of setting out a formal letter and these are constantly changing, particularly as we use computers and word-processors more and more. Even so, some conventions remain unchanged and you need to make sure you use these whenever you are required to write a formal letter.

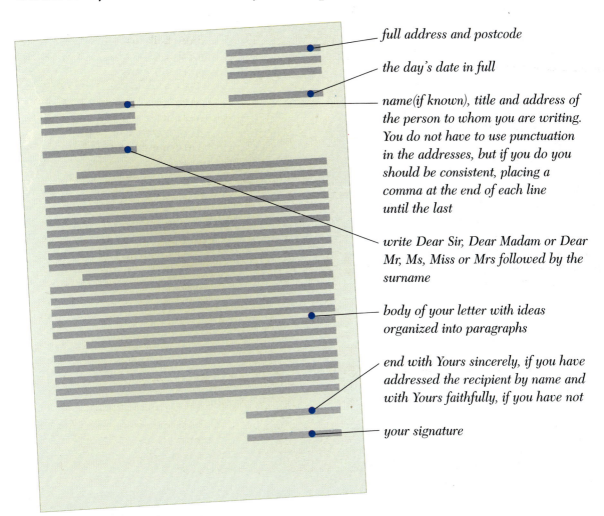

full address and postcode

the day's date in full

name(if known), title and address of the person to whom you are writing. You do not have to use punctuation in the addresses, but if you do you should be consistent, placing a comma at the end of each line until the last

write Dear Sir, Dear Madam or Dear Mr, Ms, Miss or Mrs followed by the surname

body of your letter with ideas organized into paragraphs

end with Yours sincerely, if you have addressed the recipient by name and with Yours faithfully, if you have not

your signature

Informal letter-writing

In an informal letter you still need to include your address and the date but not the name and address of the person to whom you are writing. You address the recipient by his or her first name or the name by which you usually call them, e.g. *Dear Ann, Dear Chris, Dear Gran*. An informal ending is usually *Best wishes, Love from*, or something similar, followed by your signature.

Getting the conventions of letter-writing right is only a small part of writing a good letter. Obviously it is what you say that is of most importance. A good letter should be clear, to the point and its tone should be appropriate to its audience and purpose. In the exam situation it is most likely that you will be asked to write a letter to a magazine, newspaper or an official body, such as the local council, expressing your opinions on a particular subject.

ACTIVITY 1

Read the letter on the opposite page written to a local newspaper on the subject of fur coats. Think about:

- the use of personal anecdote – 'Some years ago, I was speaking to...'

- the inclusion of facts to support the argument, e.g.'... one coat can cause the death of 12 baby ocelots, or 15 lynx, or 40 foxes, or 65 mink, or 60 rabbits.'

- the use of **rhetorical questions**, e.g. 'How can anyone presume to claim their warmth demands such a terrible sacrifice, especially when luxurious fake furs are available?'

- the use of emotive language, e.g.'Farm factories are another *evil*', '*heartrending* engravings', '*poor* creatures.'

By using these stylistic techniques the writer aims both to make her letter more interesting to the readers and to persuade them to a particular point of view.

Fur coat's high price

SOME years ago, I was speaking to a self-professed animal lover, by whose calling (nursing) one would expect compassion to be second nature.

She was wearing a fur coat. When I expressed horror at this she protested, "but I feel the cold so much. It'll be my last one!" She ignored the fact that, through her, it was the last of life itself for many animals, as just one coat can cause the death of 12 baby ocelots, or 15 lynx, or 40 foxes, or 65 mink, or 60 rabbits.

How can anyone presume to claim their warmth demands such a terrible sacrifice, especially when luxurious fake furs are available?

The two main forms of fur-bearing animal exploitation are trapping and factory-farming. Both methods are so vile, that one wonders how anyone can bear to wear the end "product."

Animals can be trapped, in excruciating agony, for days, before the trapper returns. The frantic, crazed-with-pain, creature in a trap, sometimes gnaws off the affected limb, to try to break free. Some animals (mainly foxes and otters) are so desperate, they shatter all their teeth on the steel traps, and their jawbones are raw and exposed.

The trapper is not willing to lose an animal which has amputated a limb, so what does he do? He fastens his traps to springy stakes which shoot up when the trap's jaws have snapped to, and the victim dangled (with no hope of escape) from one leg, until either its death or the return of the trapper.

Snakes, crocodiles and lizards are often skinned alive, and all for the sake of a hand-bag or shoes – a status symbol.

Farm factories are another evil. There, mink (which favour a solitary life, and space) are reared intensively, crammed two or three into a cage, which has a floor of thin wire mesh – the cages stretching in interminable rows, all exposed to winter's stormy blast, so the fur will grow faster.

I remember seeing one of Bewick's heartrending engravings, of a skeletal horse, "waiting for death". These factory-farmed creatures, too await death – by injecting, gassing, electrocution, or having their necks wrung.

Foxes, also, spend their lives shuffling backwards and forwards, in stereotyped fashion in small cages. Silver foxes are mated in February or March, and the cubs are born 51 days later, reared in those cages and killed in their first winter.

There's not even a brief taste of the wild for these poor creatures.

A badge defines it all: "Fur coats are worn by beautiful animals – and ugly people."

How True!

**Miss E D IRVING
Park Avenue
Hexham**

THE JOURNAL

ACTIVITY 2

Write a letter to a local newspaper expressing your opinion on a subject about which you feel strongly.

Before writing you need to plan your ideas carefully. Try to use some of the same techniques the writer of the sample letter uses.

POINTS to remember

- There are specific conventions of letter-writing which you need to know and use.
- A good letter should be clear, to the point and appropriate to its audience and purpose.
- By using specific stylistic techniques you can make your letters more interesting and effective.

Writing leaflets, advice sheets and news-sheets

Walk into any Careers Office and you will find an endless array of leaflets and news-sheets informing you about different occupations, offering you advice about how to choose your future career and telling you about the changes that are taking place in the world of work. If you go to your doctor's surgery you will find information on a wide range of health matters, again produced in the form of leaflets, advice sheets and news-sheets.

In every area of modern life we are surrounded by information produced in this way. The main purpose of leaflets, advice sheets and news-sheets is to give information in a quick, clear and interesting way. Leaflets and advice sheets tend to focus on one particular subject, such as the dangers of smoking, whereas a news-sheet is designed to give you an update on recent events. So a charity might produce a leaflet in order to encourage you to contribute to a particular cause but would use a news-sheet to update its members on its latest achievements.

ACTIVITY 1

Look at the three sample pieces, 'What would you kill for' (pages 81–82), 'Info news file' (page 83) and 'Your children and drugs' (page 84), and for each one answer these questions:

- Would you call this a leaflet, an advice sheet or a news-sheet? Why?

- Who is the intended audience?

- What is the intended purpose?

- What information is given to you?

- What can you say about the way the information is presented and its effectiveness?

A1

WHAT WOULD YOU KILL FOR?

A2

SO WHY DO WE DO IT?

● *I drive fast because I'm in a hurry*

The difference between driving 50 miles at 60mph and at 70mph is a saving of seven minutes. On an average journey you will probably save less than a couple of minutes by driving like a maniac. Is it worth it?

● *I have fast reflexes so I can drive faster*

Accidents are avoided by anticipation, not reaction. The reaction of a fighter pilot is only 0.4 seconds faster than that of the average driver.

● *It's slow drivers who cause accidents, getting in the way*

The one causing the accident is you, trying to overtake at any price.

● *I have to keep up with the traffic*

Driving too close causes at least 10% of accidents. Give yourself room to react.

● *I've been driving fast for years and never had an accident*

You've been lucky. Nearly 80,000 casualties every year thought it couldn't happen to them.

A3

A4

● *I only speed when there's no other traffic around*

In nearly 20% of accidents where drivers and passengers are killed or seriously injured, no other vehicle is involved.

● *There's no point in keeping to the thirty limit. If someone steps out in front of you there's nothing you can do.*

The slower you are going when you hit the brakes, the better the chance a pedestrian will have. Nine out of ten people - even children - survive a 20mph collision, but at 40mph nine out of ten are killed.

SO WHAT IS A SAFE SPEED?

Speed limits in the table overleaf are the MAXIMUM safe driving speeds for the type of road and if we all kept to them many lives would be saved.

But driving at a safe speed means more than just obeying speed limits. That may still be too fast in some road conditions, especially wet, slippery surfaces and poor visibility.

In traffic, leave a gap of at least two seconds between you and the car in front. Double the space if the road is wet or icy, or in mist and fog.

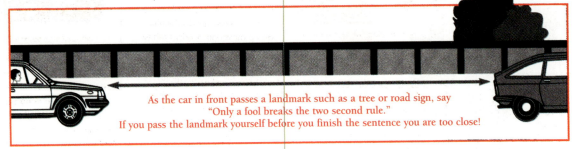

As the car in front passes a landmark such as a tree or road sign, say
"Only a fool breaks the two second rule."
If you pass the landmark yourself before you finish the sentence you are too close!

On country roads, take the bends slowly. Your car may corner well, but you don't know what's round the corner.

Slow down in residential areas.

SPEED KILLS.....KILL YOUR SPEED.

GRADUATES FACE NEW TEST

35,000 graduates are expected to qualify this year and many will find it easier to get the right job as a result of a new nation-wide computerised test which will profile and grade students' business skills and acumen.

Called the **GET** (Graduate Employability Test), it aims to establish a national benchmark, providing employers with clear and accurate information about a graduate's employability.

Pre-launch, employers such as Mercedes and Club 21 already endorse the test.

For the first time, all UK students will be able to choose to sit a unique test which will grade their computer literacy, business awareness and profile their personality – telling potential employers whether they are leaders, team workers and able to obtain results from the first day.

The test has taken over 2 years to develop by a consortium of educationalists and industrialists including the Business and Technology Council (BTEC). Sylvan Prometric, National Computing Council (NCC) and Saville and Holdsworth.

GET, the largest public test of its kind has come about as a direct result of advances in computer technology. Now employers will be able to select who they want to interview, based on information

about an applicant's business skills and aptitudes rather than just on a degree or CV alone.

Graduates will sit the GET at test centres around the country. They will be profiled and graded and then given a certificate which they can send to employers. No two candidates will receive the same questions, as alternatives of an equivalent value will be pulled out of question banks.

The man leading the consortium behind the GET, **Jonathan Brill**, tells *Inform*, 'Increasingly both employers and industries are now looking for personal qualities and business capabilities rather than just degree results. They are looking for applicants who are good at working in teams, – things a degree alone cannot guarantee.

The launch of the new GET management and human resource function will have a consistent and more objective criterion for selecting candidates for interview'.

The GET was field tested during 1996 and will be launched next month, GET should also enable up-to-date national statistics on employability to be compiled.

TOP OF THE CLASS

Middlesbrough College recently passed a thorough inspection by the FEFC, coming out with flying colours.

The college gained high grades in all aspects of its work, with the Hairdressing and Beauty provision being awarded a grade 1 (one of only ten nationally) reinforcing its reputation as a regional centre of excellence.

The percentage of grades 2 and above given, places the college firmly in the top 25% of colleges inspected nationally since 1993. The report noted 'the high overall standard of teaching in classroom and practical sessions' and the high level of achievement of all students.

Inspectors observed 217 learning sessions, and their view was that the overall standard of teaching was high. 68% of the classes observed achieved the very highest grades. The inspections covered all subjects at 'A' level, GNVQ, NVQ, basic education and professional levels, both for full-time and part-time students. Such teaching provisions led to outstanding success among the students, with a new record of 261 students progressing on to university in 1996.

The staff of the College have also been highly commended for their commitment and dedication, with the report being very positive about the close links with industry, local schools and other institutions which the college has developed and the extensive range of both general and vocational education provision that allows access for a wide range of abilities.

SETTING NEW STANDARDS

The launch of a £2 million investment package took place in Billingham recently, with the opening of The Purvis Building, Cleveland Training Centre's new £600,000 facility.

The Centre, owned by the Engineering and Marine Training Authority (EMTA), chose to name its new 130 place training facility in honour of **Bill Purvis**, Chairman of the board of advisers and a Cleveland Training Centre associate for over 25 years.

Bill Purvis, Chairman EMTA

Dr Mike Sanderson, Chief Executive of EMTA, confirmed that £2 million will be invested in the Leeholme Road site over the next five years, primarily to help overcome the North East's skills shortage and to train people specifically for the changing needs of existing and incoming industry.

David Jeffcock, the Centre's Managing Director, is confident that the investment will help CTC set new standards for training in the area.

The opening ceremony, conducted by **Mr Davey Hall**, leader of the Engineering and Electrical Union, was attended by over 60 guests including the Lord Mayor of Stockton and leading business and industry representatives.

B ▲

YOUR CHILDREN & DRUGS
MAGIC MUSHROOMS

MAGIC MUSHROOMS (or 'Shrooms as they are more commonly called) are likely to be found in fields and parks. They can be taken raw, but are usually dried and made into tea or cooked. It is illegal to prepare them in any way. The effects take around 20 minutes to occur. This effect is called a 'trip' and lasts 6–9 hours. Once it's started it can't be stopped.

Magic Mushrooms affect the mind, and alter perception of sight and sound. The effects of a 'trip' can vary depending on the user's mood. If they're feeling low, the chances of having a bad 'trip' could be increased.

Hallucinations may occur. A strong 'trip' may cause someone to see, hear, feel and taste things that aren't there. This could be frightening.

It's difficult to know how strong a dose of Magic Mushrooms will be. It is easy to take too much.

It is easy to pick the wrong type of mushroom. They all look fairly similar. Taking something that looks like a Magic Mushroom could be lethal.

Flashbacks can occur any time after the original 'trip'. Even if the original wasn't bad, the flashback could be an absolute nightmare.

Whilst 'tripping', the user could experience nausea, sickness and even vomiting.

The risks of taking Magic Mushrooms could be increased if they are taken with other drugs or alcohol.

Tell-tale signs. If your child seems moody, distant and tired don't jump to conclusions. This could be perfectly innocent. Somebody who is 'tripping' is easy to spot. They could appear restless or anxious. If you think your child has taken Magic Mushrooms it's important to stay calm and be supportive. Do what you can to make sure they're safe. When you're certain the 'trip' has stopped, that's the time to talk.

What can you do? Don't panic and don't lose your temper. Talk to them about why they took them. Most young people try drugs out of curiosity or because they're forbidden. The risk makes it seem exciting. They could be under pressure at school, or it may be an escape route from other problems.

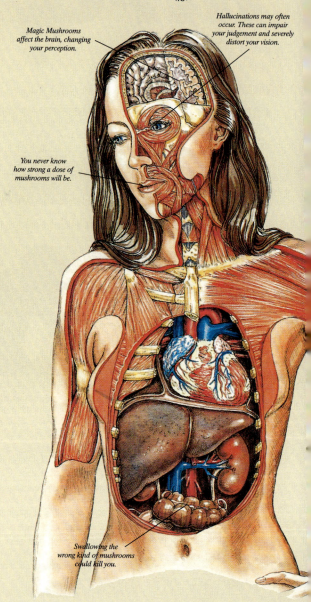

Magic Mushrooms affect the brain, changing your perception.

Hallucinations may often occur. These can impair your judgement and severely distort your vision.

You never know how strong a dose of mushrooms will be.

Swallowing the wrong kind of mushrooms could kill you.

Whatever the reason, the best way to help is to listen to them and discuss things calmly using accurate information. It's a good idea to call and talk it over with us on the number below, or alternatively ask for a copy of our 'Parents' Guide'. We'll be able to tell you more about Magic Mushrooms, more about the dangers and how you can go about helping. All calls are free and confidential.

National drugs helpline 0800 776600

ACTIVITY 2

Would a leaflet, advice sheet or news-sheet be most appropriate for each of the following? Why?

- Details on the events and successes of a school's term.
- Information on how to diet without endangering your health.
- A summary of a local council's recent work for residents.
- Information for tourists visiting an area for the first time.

You may be asked to write a leaflet, advice sheet or news-sheet in your English exam. This is a difficult thing to do properly as you have to be very selective about the material you choose to include. You must make sure that you identify the audience and purpose accurately and that you give careful thought to how you present your ideas.

Aim to keep your layout as clear and straightforward as possible. As you are writing by hand it is probably best *not* to attempt to write in columns.

ACTIVITY 3

Choose one activity from the following:

1 Write a news-sheet for young people moving into your area informing them of things to do and places to go to.

2 Write an advice sheet for incoming Year 7 (11–12 years) pupils suggesting how they should get the best out of their time at your school.

3 Write a leaflet for pupils in your own year which aims to persuade them to support a charity of your choice.

Before writing you should plan your ideas carefully. Here are some pointers to help you:

- identify your audience and purpose
- list the information you want to include
- reorganize it into the most appropriate order
- decide on a suitable heading and sub-headings
- decide whether a diagram would be useful – if so, keep it simple and annotate it clearly
- decide on what tone is best suited to your audience and purpose
- consider whether any of the following would be appropriate or useful: an easily remembered slogan, highlighting, the use of bold print, underlining, rhetorical questions, a helpline number or address for further information.

POINTS to remember

- Leaflets, advice sheets and news-sheets are intended to inform the reader in a quick, clear and interesting way.
- Good organization and clear layout of information are essential.
- Use presentational features which are effective and relevant but do not spend too much time on these.

How to approach Paper 1 Section B

In this section of the exam you are given a choice of **writing** tasks from which you should choose one. The type of writing tested here is writing which argues, persuades or instructs, although the tasks are not necessarily separated into these categories. So you might find, for example, that a single task requires you to do more than one of these things and possibly all three.

The exam practice questions on the following pages are linked to the same topics or themes as the non-fiction materials used in the Section A exam practice papers (pages 40–52). It would, therefore, be a good idea to remind yourself of the materials used in Section A before starting to work on Section B. Your teacher will tell you which tier you should focus on.

Once you have looked at the Section A materials you are ready to read the tasks set for Section B.

Making your choice and planning your ideas

Often candidates do not give sufficient thought to their **choice** of task. It is important that you choose the one which gives you most scope to write in an interesting and informative way. For example, there is not much point choosing to write about how the environment affects the way we live if you have few ideas and no strong feelings on this subject. Read all the options carefully and consider what you could write about for each one.

Once you have made your choice, start by writing the instructions at the top of your page. In the exam you should spend at least ten minutes planning your piece of writing. For these practice questions it will probably take you a bit longer. Remember that these planning notes are for your own benefit to help you produce a well-structured and logical piece of writing. You will not be directly assessed on your plan in the exam but without it you are less likely to produce a good piece of writing. The 'examiner comments' section on pages 89–90 takes you through the stages you should go through before starting to write your answer.

Exam Practice – Foundation Tier

PAPER 1 SECTION B

Answer *one* question in this section.

- You can use some of the information from Section A if you want to, but you do not have to do so.
- Spend *about one hour* on this section.

1   Write a letter to a magazine for teenagers about a town or area you know well. You should aim to persuade the readers that this place is worth visiting.

2   **It is the people not the place that matter.**

Write an article for a local newspaper expressing your views on this subject.

3   Write a leaflet for visitors to your area, or one you know well, introducing them to the places of interest.

Exam Practice – Higher Tier

PAPER 1 SECTION B

Answer *one* question in this section.

- You can use some of the information from Section A if you want to, but you do not have to do so.
- Spend *about one hour* on this section.

1   Your home town, or area, has been criticized on your local radio station. Write a letter in reply, arguing that it is a good place to live in and to visit.

2   **How our environment affects the way we live.**

Write an article for a local newspaper using this as your headline. You might like to think about several different types of environment.

3   Write a visitors' guide to a well-known High Street. It can be based on a real or imagined place and can be serious or humorous.

The examiner comments ...

The following stages should be carried out before answering any of the
questions from either Tier. The first task on the Foundation Tier is used as
an example here.

> Write a letter to a magazine for teenagers about a town or area you
> know well. You should aim to persuade the readers that this place is
> worth visiting.

Stage 1 – *Identify your audience, purpose and form*

Audience: teenage magazine readers.
Purpose: to persuade them that a particular town or area is worth visiting.
Form: write a letter.

Stage 2 – *Gather ideas*

Jot down as many ideas as you can think of that are relevant to the task.
Your list might look something like this:

size of town	*community spirit*	*arts*
access to other places	*what it means to me*	*housing*
cinemas	*nightlife*	*architecture*
High Street	*sports facilities*	*football club*
shops	*at different times of year*	*famous people*
the people	*surrounding area*	*transport*
the schools	*compared to other places*	*library*

Stage 3 – *Start to link your ideas together into groups*

Some will no longer seem appropriate and others may occur to you as you do
this. Give each group of ideas a general title.

Personal: what it means to me – community spirit – the people –
                     compare to other places

Places to go: High Street (shops & architecture) – sports facilities –
                     cinema – football club – nightlife

Physical features: where it is – size – surrounding area – access to other places

Other: at different times of year (bustling with visitors in summer;
                     quieter in winter)

Stage 4 – *Order your ideas*

You now have several groups of ideas that will form the basis of your writing.
These need to be placed in the order in which you are going to write about
them. You should make sure you can move easily from one group to another.
These groups could form the basis of your paragraphs.

1 Physical features

2 Places to go

3 At different times of the year

4 Personal

Stage 5 – *Think about expression*

Now that you have decided what will make up the main body of your piece of writing you need to think about how you are going to express your ideas. Ask yourself the following questions:

● Should the tone be formal or informal?

● Should I write in the first or the third person?

● How should I adjust my vocabulary and sentence structures to suit my purpose and audience?

For this task the answers are likely to be that the tone should be informal; it should be written in the first person; and the vocabulary should aim to persuade and should target a teenage audience.

Stage 6 – *Think about form*

Lastly, think about the form that your writing is to take. Ask yourself how the form will affect the way you present your ideas. Look back at earlier sections in this book to remind yourself of specific features of letters, leaflets and articles. Use what you have learnt about presentation to make your writing as interesting and appropriate as you can.

Once you have worked your way through these preparatory stages you are ready to write your response.

Checking and revising your writing

Always reserve five minutes at the end of your exam for checking and correcting your work. This should not be confused with redrafting, which is the process of reorganizing, improving and re-writing which you will be familiar with in coursework. In the few minutes you have you should aim to carefully read through what you have written. It's very easy to see what you **think** you have written, so try to avoid this by allowing each word on the page to register in your head, as though you were reading it out loud. Be on the lookout for errors in punctuation and spelling, particularly in the areas where you know you tend to make mistakes. Where you can see ways of improving what you've written, by adding or deleting certain words, or changing the punctuation, do so, but take great care to make sure each sentence as a whole still makes sense.

Sample Paper 1 – Foundation Tier

Time

- 2 hours

Instructions to candidates

- Answer *Question 1* from Section A and *one* question from Section B.
- You must *not* use a dictionary in this exam.

SECTION A

- Read **It's easy to be green** and **The green revolution loses pace** and answer *all* parts of the question that follows.
- Spend *about one hour* on this section.

1 a)   i List three opinions from **It's easy to be green**.
         ii List three facts from **The green revolution loses pace**.

   b)   Why, according to the writer of **The green revolution loses pace**, are shoppers turning their backs on environmentally friendly products?

         Give as many reasons as you can in your answer.

   c)   Both pieces are concerned with green issues. Which do you think is likely to have the greatest impact on its readers' attitudes? Give clear reasons for your choice.

         In your answer you should comment on:
         - what they are about
         - the different ways the ideas are presented
         - the language used in both pieces
         - your own response.

16

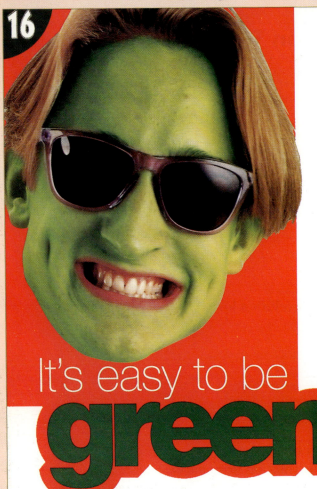

It's easy to be
green

Yes, we're finally getting the message that the environment really matters. And, as well as all the hard work by organisations such as Friends of the Earth and the British Trust for Conservation Volunteers, we are all finding it easier to be green. However, if you still think you could do a bit more for caring for the environment, then read on.

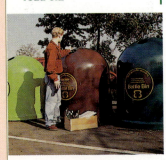

AT HOME

It's so convenient to throw away all our rubbish in the same bin. Unfortunately, when we do this it makes it difficult to sort out and recycle, and it ends up being thrown on one huge rubbish tip. In some cases this can lead to a build up of poisonous gases which, as well as the possibility of exploding, can also wash down through the soil and pollute local water supplies. However, these problems can easily be solved by sorting your own rubbish out and disposing of it appropriately.

But first, before you rush out and empty the dustbin, make sure your mum or dad are happy about doing this. There are many towns now which have recycling bins where your family can dispose of their rubbish more usefully. Plus, there are some councils who will collect different types of material, such as paper and tins, from your home. Check out first which items they recycle and how best to pack them. Your parents will be happier to help you out if you show them that you've looked into recycling. Also think about where you can store these items at home before you dispose of them i.e. in the garage or shed, for example.

STORING RECYCLABLE ITEMS

Paper An ideal way to store paper is in a strong cardboard box.

Here's what to do:
- Make a short nick in the middle of each side of the box.
- Lay two pieces of string across the box, tuck the ends into the cuts leaving a fairly long length of string hanging down the outsides.
- When the box is nearly full of newspapers tie the string tightly and remove for recycling.
- Repeat the same procedure for your next lot of papers.

You can also follow this procedure for cardboard boxes such as cereal packets. Just remember to flatten the boxes first.

Tins All cans are recyclable. However, some recycling skips may ask you to separate steel from aluminium cans. How can you tell which is which? Well, test the can with a magnet. If it is attracted you know it's not aluminium.

Glass Bottles An old bottle crate is an ideal way to store and carry glass. Just remember that most bottle banks like you to sort the bottles out by colour first and do not want metal caps included.

Plastics Find out if your supermarket collects plastic drink bottles for recycling. If not, they will have to be thrown away with the rubbish. You can still collect them in a cardboard box, flattening them first to reduce the amount of space they take up.

Clothes Old clothes can be taken to your local charity shop, but please make sure they are cleaned first. Anything else, put in black bin liners in readiness for your next jumble sale. And, with a bit of luck, there won't be that much rubbish left to go in the dustbin.

If you are interested in recycling, write to your council to find out what schemes are available. Some councils even have a recycling officer who will be able to give good advice. Look in your local telephone directory for the number. Don't forget to ask permission from the person who pays the bill before you use the phone.

The green revolution loses pace

By David Norris

SHOPPERS are turning their back on the green revolution.

Faced with new concerns, such as food safety, they are increasingly shunning environment-friendly products and going back to cheaper conventional varieties.

The slump in demand for goods ranging from washing powders to hairsprays is causing supermarkets to reduce their ranges of ecology-conscious goods.

Many high street chains have already ditched some of the pioneer green products brought in on the back of rising environmental awareness in the late Eighties.

These include the washing powder Ecover and the Ark range of detergents, supported by celebrities such as Paul McCartney.

Sainsbury's has dropped the fabric conditioner and washing powder products from its own-brand 'Green Care' range.

Tesco is reviewing the selection at its stores and the Co-operative Wholesale Society has scrapped its Environmental Care products.

The main reasons for the mass consumer defection appear to be tight family budgets and job insecurity. Green products cost an average of 15 to 20 per cent more.

Analysts said public awareness had been diverted from ecological concerns into other areas, such as food scares and world problems.

John Elkington, of the environmental consultants Sustainability, said issues such as Bosnia appeared to have taken priority.

Sainsbury's said yesterday that sales of Green Care products had been declining for some time. But a spokesman pointed out that the store's standard products were offering similar levels of environmental protection without the special label.

'We do not believe that people are turning away from the environment – the standard products we offer are now much better,' she said.

Neil Verlander, of Friends of the Earth, said shoppers were confused about whether they really were helping the environment by buying specially-marked products.

He called for an official labelling system to show exactly how eco-friendly products were.

A National Consumer Council report last month said some manufacturers were cashing in on the public's environmental concerns with 'misleading, meaningless and downright dishonest' claims.

Some fridge and aerosol products advertise the fact that they are CFC-free, when such gases – which can damage the Earth's protective ozone layer – have already been banned by the Government.

'To claim green credentials as a result of not using a banned product is arguably misleading,' the NCC study said.

"I have a green soul but my bank account is in the red!"

DAILY MAIL

SECTION B

Answer *one* question in this section.

- You can use some of the information from Section A if you want to, but you do not have to do so.
- Spend *about one hour* on this section.

2   Write a letter to your local council about recycling. You should:
- point out the importance of recycling
- suggest ways the council could improve on the provision it makes for this
- show how this would be good for the environment and the council.

3   Write an article for a school magazine which argues that pupils and staff should give more thought to the environment. Write about the school environment *and* other relevant issues.

4   Write an advice sheet for 16-year-olds on one of the following subjects:
- coping with parents
- preparing for exams
- how to be more healthy.

Sample Paper 1 – Higher Tier

Time

- 2 hours

Instructions to candidates

- Answer *Question 1* from Section A and *one* question from Section B.
- You must *not* use a dictionary in this exam.

SECTION A

- Read **Rhinoceros** and **Taking a Picture** and answer *all* parts of the question that follows.
- Spend *about one hour* on this section.

1 a) List *two* facts and *two* opinions from *each* of the pieces.

   b) i List five points in the leaflet which might persuade the reader to join WWF.

      ii Write about the way the ideas are presented in this leaflet.

      In your answer you should refer to:
- the layout
- the organization of the text
- variations in print
- illustrations
- any other features which you consider to be relevant.

   c) The two extracts tell us very different things about rhinos.

     Write about the way rhinos are portrayed in **Taking a Picture** and compare this with their portrayal in **Rhinoceros**.

Rhinoceros

Fighting for Nature

WWF

information

Rhinoceros

Rhino numbers have plummeted from 72,000 animals to only 11,000 in just 22 years. They are killed for their horns, which are used in Oriental medicine or carved into dagger handles.

1

2

Current threats and problems

Trade in rhino horn or its by-products is banned under CITES (the Convention on International Trade in Endangered Species) signed by more than 120 countries. But poaching and illegal trading continues.

Rhino horn has been a medicinal ingredient in China for at least 4,600 years. Throughout the Far East it is used to treat fevers, rheumatism, arthritis and even strokes. In some places, such as Taiwan, African rhino horn is considered to be less potent and valuable that Asian rhino horn.

Apart from poaching. Asian rhinos have also suffered from loss of their rainforest and marshland habitat mainly due to human settlement and expanding agriculture. They once ranged widely across south and south-east Asia but are now found only in small isolated areas – and are prone to extinction because of the small number of breeding adults.

WWF's work

WWF funds over 30 rhino projects, including crucial work done by TRAFFIC (WWF's highly effective wildlife trade monitoring programme) to stamp out the illegal trade in the Far East and promote alternatives to the medicinal trade in rhino horn. This is easier said than done: the organisation has to treat people's traditional beliefs with respect, and lifetime customs are difficult to change.

WWF also funds projects to protect rhinos in the wild such as assisting anti-poaching efforts, captive breeding programmes, habitat protection and translocating rhinos from vulnerable areas to safe havens.

Background and specific projects

There are five species of rhino – each threatened with extinction even though some are actually increasing in numbers. The Javan, Sumatran and Indian rhino live in Asia; the black and white in Africa. The Javan rhino is one of the rarest large mammals in the world, with fewer than 100 surviving in the Ujong Kulon National Park in West Java and in Vietnam. WWF has a long-term project

3

to conserve the rhinos in Ujung Kulon and to strengthen Vietnam's protected areas.

WWF is preparing a plan to protect the 500 remaining Sumatran or woolly rhinos, as well as supporting the Kerinci-Seblat National Park in West Sumatra.

The Indian rhino population has risen from a dozen in 1908 to around 2,000 today. This success is due to protection provided by nine reserves set up primarily to conserve the tiger more than 20 years ago. There are now 19 tiger reserves in India, many of which have been expanded and upgraded.

In Africa, poaching has been so ruthless and unrelenting that black rhino numbers have plummeted from 60,000 to 2,500 in just 20 years – a matter of enormous concern to conservationists. But there is a glimmer of good news from that continent: at the end of the last century the southern white rhino was believed to be extinct. However, a small population was discovered in South Africa and after careful protection it has expanded to some 5,900 animals. The northern white rhino lives only in Zaire's Garamba National Park. In 1983 there were a mere 12 animals – but now, as a result of a major WWF conservation project, they have increased to over 30.

Rhinoceros

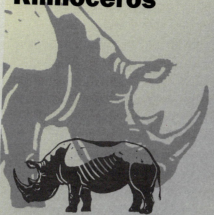

What you can do

WWF depends on public support morally and financially to carry out urgent conservation projects to save the rhino and other species and habitats facing extinction. Please help us continue our vital work by becoming a member, making a donation, joining a supporters group or by buying some of our specially selected merchandise from our free gift catalogue. For further information please contact:

WWF, Panda House, Weyside Park, Godalming, Surrey GU7 1XR Telephone 01483 426444

4

Fighting for Nature

From its earliest days back in 1961, WWF has been committed to saving threatened wildlife species and their habitats.

That fundamental principle is still one of the great driving forces behind the organisation – though our remit at home and abroad had broadened considerably in the 33 years since our inauguration.

WWF conserves nature by protecting wild species in wild places, by promoting and practising the sustainable use of biological resources, and by creating a better educated and more aware public that can take enlightened decisions about lifestyles and consumption.

As we head towards the new millennium, WWF will pursue these fundamental tasks as part of its ultimate goal – to stop the accelerating degradation of the natural environment, and to build a future in which people live in harmony with nature.

WWF UK (World Wide Fund For Nature)
Panda House, Weyside Park, Godalming, Surrey GU7 1XR
Telephone 01483 426444 Fax 01483 426409
Registered Charity Number 201707.

Printed on recycled paper. November 1994

TAKING A PICTURE

Leaving Lembogi, Kabechi and the old guide behind, I took Asani with the cameras and ran down the slope, crossed the bog and climbed up the far side. Mohamed was to follow at a short distance, on account of the clatter of his boots on the rocks. I drew to within forty yards of the rhino, yet they still looked like a couple of grey boulders as they browsed off an isolated patch of sere grass. The bleached stalks bowing before the wind alone gave a flicker of life to that adamantine expanse of stone.

The wind had risen to a tearing gale, and nosing straight into it I approached the rhino somewhat downhill. There was no chance of this steady blow jumping round to betray me, and it was strong enough to carry away any sound of my footsteps. Precaution was therefore unnecessary and I walked boldly up to them. Just how close I was, it is hard to say; but I felt that I could have flipped a pebble at them, and I noted subconsciously that the eye of the one nearest me was not dark brown as I imagined it, but the colour of sherry.

And the experience has left me in some doubt whether a rhino has such poor eye sight as is commonly believed. Perhaps they heard the clicking of the cinema camera. This may have given the nearer one my direction, and then my coat or the brim of my hat flapping in the wind possibly caught his eye. At any rate, his ears pricked up, his champing jaws were held in suspense, and that little pale eye was very definitely focused straight upon me.

He lifted his head, trying to catch the wind. It told him nothing, but he now came deliberately towards me, nose to the ground and horn foremost, full of suspicion. I pressed the button and tried to keep a steady hand. This was not easy; for a rhino seen through the finder of a small cinema camera looks remote, and it is only when you take the camera down to make sure, that you are horribly startled to see how near he really is. In the finder I saw his tail go up, and knew that he was on the point of charging. Though it was the impression of a fraction of a second, it was unforgettable. He was standing squarely upon a flat boulder that raised him like a pedestal, and he seemed to tower up rugged and clear-cut as a monument against the flying clouds.

Such a chance could never possibly occur again, and the magnificence of that picture for the moment blinded me to all else. I had done better to bolt then, while he was still hesitating. I read the danger signal, yet in a kind of trance of excitement I still held the camera against my forehead. Then Mohamed fired a shot over the rhino's head to scare him, and I turned and fled for my very life.

The rhino was only momentarily taken aback. Before I had time to skip out of his sight he had made up his mind to charge me. The angry thunder of his snort, mingled with a screech like an engine blowing off steam, lent me wings. When I dared throw a glance over my shoulder I saw that both rhino were bearing down upon me with frightening speed. The boys had had a start of me, and as I raced after them across the vistas of stone bare as asphalt without a blade of cover anywhere, conviction swept over me that this time the game was up.

Though I ran and ran as I had never run in my life before, and my heart pounded in my ears and my lungs stiffened with the pain of drawing breath, time went suddenly into slow motion. Each step was weighted with lead; I wanted to fly over the ground and, as in some horrid nightmare, I felt as though I were scarcely moving.

The rhino were swiftly gaining upon me; their furious snorts overtook me on the wings of the gale. The boys, on the other hand, had disappeared as though the earth had swallowed them. I made one more desperate spurt and then, as I realised the utter futility of it, a fold in the hillside opened to receive me also. I tumbled headlong down a little cliff and landed on a ledge of heather.

The rhino would never face this drop even if they looked over and saw me. I glanced up apprehensively, but there was no sign of them.

In this sheltered place there was not a sound, and even the wind had dropped. With thankful heart I stretched myself face downward on the heather, and panted as though I could never get a complete lungful of air again, while waves of crimson and orange rushed and throbbed before my eyes.

The boys climbed up to me (they had landed farther down) and seeing Mohamed's lugubrious expression of disapproval I quickly put my word in first.

"That," said I, "is the best picture I have ever taken!"

SPEAK TO THE EARTH: WANDERINGS AND REFLECTIONS AMONG ELEPHANTS AND MOUNTAINS BY VIVIENNE DE WATTEVILLE

SECTION B

Answer *one* question in this section.

- You can use some of the information from Section A if you want to, but you do not have to do so.
- Spend *about one hour* on this section.

2   Write a leaflet for Year 7 pupils (aged 11–12 years) about the rhinoceros and the threat to its survival. Aim to persuade the pupils to adopt the WWF as their year charity.

3   Write an article for a nature magazine about an animal, or animals, of your choice. You should aim to:
- inform your reader about the animal(s)
- encourage a greater interest in them.

4   Should people support animal charities when there are so many children in need? Write a letter to your local newspaper giving your views on this subject.

PAPER 2

*This paper examines **Reading** in Section A and **Writing** in Section B. Each section is worth 15% of your final mark for English.*

Section A requires a reading response to prepared poetry. The poetry appears as part of the **NEAB Anthology**, consisting of a selection from the work of three poets in the English literary tradition together with a selection of poems from other cultures and traditions.

Section B requires one piece of writing which informs, explains or describes; some of the tasks will be linked thematically to poems in the **Anthology**.

Section A

This is a test of the prepared reading from the **Anthology** which you will be studying in school. The English section is divided into two parts:

- Part 1 – the work of three poets in the English literary tradition
- Part 2 – a selection of poems from other cultures and traditions.

In your exam you will be asked to answer one question on one of the three poets and one question on the poems from other cultures and traditions. You will be offered a choice of questions in both parts.

The Assessment Objectives, which form the basis of the NEAB Mark Scheme, are based on your ability to:

- read with insight and engagement
- make appropriate reference to text
- develop and sustain interpretations of text
- follow an argument
- select material appropriate to purpose
- make cross references
- understand and evaluate linguistic devices
- understand and evaluate structural and presentational devices
- comment on ways language varies/changes.

How this section helps

This section uses a wide variety of poems from different times and places. It does not use poems from a specific anthology (NEAB will change their Anthologies every two to three years). Rather it uses a range of poems to teach you the *skills* you need to apply to reading the poems in the anthology you are using. You should then use those skills to help you in your study of your anthology texts.

Understanding the text

You shouldn't worry if you don't understand a poem the first time you read it. Many good poems are not fully understood on a first reading by anyone. It may take several attempts before the reader understands what is being said and starts to appreciate the craft of the poet. Poems often have different layers of meaning which need to be unwrapped.

You may be surprised by how much you get out of a poem after a number of readings. Some poems will stay in your mind forever and at some future point an event or experience may trigger your memory to bring that poem to mind again.

ACTIVITY 1

Read the poem on page 105 several times, preferably aloud, before answering the questions below:

1 The poet recalls a particular incident in which his son was hurt. Trace the sequence of events. The first two are done for you below:

The poet's son fell in the nettle bed and was upset

The parents soothed him

2 Look at the way the poet describes the nettles;

those green spears,
That regiment of spite,
that fierce parade,
the fallen dead,
tall recruits

What can you say about the images the poet uses to describe the nettles? Why do you think he uses these kinds of images?

3 What does the poet feel about the nettles? How does he respond to them?

4 What words would you use to describe the poet's feelings for his son?

5 This poem is not just about the incident with the nettles. The poet ends the poem with the line, 'My son would often feel sharp wounds again'. What do you think he means by this?

6 What do you think he has learnt from his 'battle' with the nettles?

7 What does the incident with the nettles represent or symbolize?

Nettles

My son aged three fell in the nettle bed.
'Bed' seemed a curious name for those green spears,
That regiment of spite behind the shed:
It was no place for rest. With sobs and tears
5   The boy came seeking comfort and I saw
White blisters beaded on his tender skin.
We soothed him till his pain was not so raw.
At last he offered us a watery grin,
And then I took my billhook, honed the blade
10   And went outside and slashed in fury with it
Till not a nettle in that fierce parade
Stood upright anymore. And then I lit
A funeral pyre to burn the fallen dead,
But in two weeks the busy sun and rain
15   Had called up tall recruits behind the shed:
My son would often feel sharp wounds again.

Vernon Scannell

ACTIVITY 2

Now read the next poem written by the same poet. Read it through once to get a feel of it and, after the second or third reading, try to answer the questions placed next to it.

Uncle Edward's affliction

Uncle Edward was colour-blind;
We grew accustomed to the fact.
When he asked someone to hand him
The green book from the window-seat
5 And we observed its bright red cover
Either apathy or tact
Stifled comment. We passed it over.
Much later, I began to wonder
What curious world he wandered in,
10 Down streets where pea-green pillar-boxes
Grinned at a fire-engine as green;
How Uncle Edward's sky at dawn
And sunset flooded marshy green.
Did he ken John Peel with his coat so green
15 And Robin Hood in Lincoln red?
On country walks avoid being stung
By nettles hot as a witch's tongue?
What meals he savoured with his eyes:
Green strawberries and fresh red peas,
20 Green beef and greener burgundy.
All unscientific, so it seems:
His world was not at all like that,
So those who claim to know have said.
Yet, I believe, in war-smashed France
25 He must have crawled from neutral mud
To lie in pastures dark and red
And seen, appalled, on every blade
The rain of innocent green blood.

Vernon Scannell

Who does 'we' refer to?

What colours does Uncle Edward confuse?
How do his relatives respond?
What was 'passed over'?
What words suggest the passage of time?

What fascinates the poet about the world he imagines his Uncle to inhabit?

What tone* does the poet use when describing this world?

Who might those 'who claim to know' be?
How does the tone change here (line 24)?

What world does the poet now imagine (lines 24–28)?

* Turn to page 129 for definition.

ACTIVITY 3

Now that you've had time to look at and think about this poem how would you answer the question, **What is it about?** Are there several answers you could give? Think about, and make notes on, the following:

- what you learn about Uncle Edward
- what you learn about the poet
- the different images of colour blindness
- the different tones.

Now try writing out your answer.

POINTS to remember

- A poem needs to be read several times, at least once aloud.
- There may be different layers of meaning which you will uncover gradually.
- Ask yourself the questions, Who? What? Where? When? How? Why? to help you get started.
- Think about the tone the poet uses and the way this affects the meaning.

Referring to the text

When you write about poetry you are expressing your own ideas. These may well be different to the ideas of the person sitting next to you or to your teacher's. There is no 'correct' interpretation of a poem, nor just one way of looking at it. Your understanding and feelings about a poem will depend on your experiences of life and the kind of person you are. Some poems will affect you more than others; some will have greater meaning for you. What is important is being able to explain your ideas and feelings. To do this you need to be able to refer to the poem to show *why* you think as you do.

ACTIVITY 1

Read the poem below carefully several times. Remember it often helps to read a poem aloud.

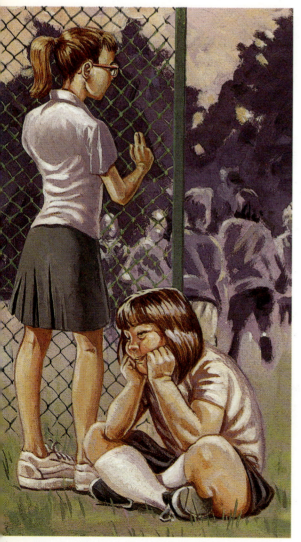

Tich Miller

Tich Miller wore glasses
with elastoplast-pink frames
and had one foot three sizes larger than the other.

When they picked two teams for outdoor games
5   she and I were always the last two
left standing by the wire-mesh fence.

We avoided one another's eyes,
stooping, perhaps, to re-tie a shoelace,
or affecting interest in the flight

10   of some fortunate bird, and pretended
not to hear the urgent conference:
'Have Tubby!' 'No, no, have Tich!'

Usually they chose me, the lesser dud,
and she lolloped, unselected,
15   to the back of the other team.

At eleven we went to different schools.
In time I learned to get my own back,
sneering at hockey-players who couldn't spell.

Tich died when she was twelve.

Wendy Cope

ACTIVITY 2

A typical question on the poem **Tich Miller** would be:

With reference to the poem, explain your thoughts and feelings about the experiences of the two girls.

In order to answer this question well you need to think carefully about the poem's meaning and the poet's use of language. Here are some suggestions to help you do this.

a) Write down your first impressions:

- What is the poem about?
- What effect does the last line of the poem have on you?

b) Pick out words or phrases from the poem that answer these questions:

- What words emphasize Tich's different appearance?
- What do the two girls do while waiting to be picked?
- Why is the bird described as 'fortunate'?

- How does the poet describe herself in verse 5?
- What word is used to describe the way Tich moves?
- How does the poet get her own back?

c) Read the advice in 'How to make references to the text' below.

d) Now try answering the question at the start of this activity, remembering to use quotations to support the points you want to make.

How to make references to the text

When writing about a poem you might refer to things in it without wanting to quote directly from the text.

e.g. The poet, Wendy Cope, describes the unpleasant experience she and another girl called Tich had while at school together. In the second verse we learn how they were always the last to be picked for the outdoor games teams.

At other times you will want to make closer reference to the actual text by quoting directly from it. You can use quotations in two different ways.

a) They can become part of your sentence as with:

Tich Miller's glasses are described as having 'elastoplast-pink frames' which makes them sound dull and ugly and quite clumsy-looking.

and:

The idea that the two girls are in some way imprisoned by 'the wire-mesh fence' is reinforced by the reference to the 'flight / of some fortunate bird'.

(*Notice how / is used to show a line break.*)

b) Longer quotations should be set out separately as with:

> Tich and the poet suffered the same humiliation and discomfort
> but they did not share their feelings or
> even communicate with each other:
>
> 'We avoided one another's eyes,
> stooping, perhaps, to re-tie a shoelace.'

and:

> Although it was obviously a painful experience for the poet
> there is a small note of triumph when she describes how she
> got the better of it:
>
> 'In time I learned to get my own back,
> sneering at hockey-players who couldn't spell.'

The tricky thing with using quotations is to make sure that they are relevant and that you don't overdo it. Too many quotations can be as bad as too few. Aim for a balance between reference to the poem, your own comments, and quotation.

POINTS *to remember*

- Poems affect people differently – there is no single 'correct' response.
- Always support your point of view by reference to the poem.
- You can refer to parts of the poem indirectly or by direct quotation.

Following an argument

Poetry is immensely varied. A poem may:

- tell a story or describe a scene or incident
- be an exploration of language in which the poet experiments with the patterns of words and their sounds
- focus on feelings or emotions, giving the reader a new insight into the experiences of others
- develop a specific argument or point of view in which the poet explains why she or he thinks this way.

In this section we focus on the development of a point of view. On pages 112 and 113 you will find two poems on the subject of work. They were written at different times but by the same poet.

ACTIVITY 1

Read the poems several times before answering these questions. Reading the poems aloud may help you to be more aware of the different tones.

Toads

- What is the poet's view of work in the first two verses?
- What examples does he use to show that it is possible to survive without work?
- What quality does he say he lacks?
- Why does he feel unable to give up work?
- What words would you use to describe the tone of the poem?

Toads Revisited

- Why does the poet think being in the park should be better than being at work?
- What kind of people are in the park?
- Why are they there?
- What is the effect of the exclamation mark in the line 'Think of being them!' (line 19).
- In what way does he now regard 'the toad work'?
- What words would you use to describe the tone of this poem?

Toads

Why should I let the toad *work*
    Squat on my life?
Can't I use my wit as a pitchfork
    And drive the brute off?

5 Six days of the week it soils
    With its sickening poison –
Just for paying a few bills!
    That's out of proportion.

Lots of folk live on their wits:
10   Lecturers, lispers,
Losels, loblolly-men, louts –
    They don't end as paupers;

Lots of folks live up lanes
    With fires in a bucket,
15 Eat windfalls and tinned sardines –
    They seem to like it.

Their nippers have got bare feet,
    Their unspeakable wives
Are skinny as whippets – and yet
20   No one actually *starves*.

Ah, were I courageous enough
    To shout *Stuff your pension*!
But I know, all too well, that's the stuff
    That dreams are made on:

25 For something sufficiently toad-like
    Squats in me, too;
Its hunkers are heavy as hard luck,
    And cold as snow,

And will never allow me to blarney
30   My way to getting
The fame and the girl and the money
    All at one sitting.

I don't say, one bodies the other
    One's spiritual truth
35 But I do say it's hard to lose either,
    When you have both.

Philip Larkin

Toads Revisited

Walking around in the park
Should feel better than work:
The lake, the sunshine,
The grass to lie on,

5 Blurred playground noises
Beyond black-stockinged nurses –
Not a bad place to be,
Yet it doesn't suit me.

Being one of the men
10 You meet of an afternoon:
Palsied old step-takers,
Hare-eyed clerks with the jitters,

Waxed-fleshed out-patients
Still vague from accidents,
15 And characters in long coats
Deep in the litter-baskets –

All dodging the toad work
By being stupid or weak.
Think of being them!
20 Hearing the hours chime,

Watching the bread delivered,
The sun by clouds covered,
The children going home;
Think of being them,

25 Turning over their failures
By some bed of lobelias.
Nowhere to go but indoors,
No friends but empty chairs –

No, give me my in-tray,
30 My loaf-haired secretary,
My shall-I-keep-the-call-in-Sir:
What else can I answer,

When the lights come on at four
At the end of another year
35 Give me your arm, old toad;
Help me down Cemetery Road.

Philip Larkin

ACTIVITY 2

Now that you have considered these two poems separately try using your ideas to compare them. Then answer the following question:

What different arguments about work does Larkin offer in **Toads** and **Toads Revisited**?

It might help to organize your points in this order:

- the attitude to work in both poems
- the evidence used to support the argument in **Toads**
- the evidence used to support the argument in **Toads Revisited**
- the main differences and/or similarities between the arguments
- the contrasting tones of the poems and how these are created
- the argument you find most convincing and why.

POINTS *to remember*

- When following an argument you need to break it down step by step.
- Think carefully about the ideas the poet uses to support his or her point of view.
- When comparing two or more poems you should focus on their similarities and differences.

Looking at language

When writing or speaking about Maths or Science you have probably got accustomed to using words like *experiment*, *formula* and *equation*. However, such words aren't much use to you unless you understand the nature of the experiment, when to use a particular formula or what the equation means. Similarly, there are words you may have been encouraged to use when writing about poetry, words like *simile**, *metaphor** and *personification**. These can be useful in helping you to describe the poet's technique, but only if they are accompanied by an understanding of what the poet has achieved by using those images. There is nothing to be gained in an exam by simply spotting similes. You have to be able to explore *why* the poet has used language in a particular way and comment on the effectiveness of a particular image. An image is like a picture painted with words. It provides a vivid description designed to move us in some way – to make us feel an emotion or to think of something in a certain way.

ACTIVITY 1

Read the following short poem carefully before answering the questions on it. The poem contains a simile in which the poet compares a sound to 'steps of passing ghosts'.

November Night

Listen …
With faint dry sound,
Like steps of passing ghosts,
The leaves, frost-crisped, break from the trees
And fall.

Adelaide Crapsey

- How does the poet invite the reader to hear what is being described?

- What is the effect of using the adjectives 'faint' and 'dry' to describe the sound?

- What simile is used in the third line of the poem? What effect does this create?

- What do the combined words 'frost-crisped' suggest to you?

- What is the effect of the word 'break' in the fourth line of the poem?

- How does the final line 'And fall' link with the image of 'passing ghosts'?

Using your answers to these questions, write a paragraph about the way the poet uses language to convey the image of **November Night**.

* Turn to page 129 for definitions

Fog

The fog comes
on little cat feet.
It sits looking
over harbor and city
on silent haunches
and then moves on.

Carl Sandburg

Extract from **The Love Song of J. Alfred Prufrock**

The yellow fog that rubs its back upon the window-panes,
The yellow smoke that rubs its muzzle on the window-panes,
Licked its tongue into the corners of the evening,
Lingered upon the pools that stand in drains,
Let fall upon its back the soot that falls from chimneys,
Slipped by the terrace, made a sudden leap,
And seeing that it was a soft October night,
Curled once about the house, and fell asleep.

T. S. Eliot

ACTIVITY 2

In the two poems above both poets use the image of a cat, in very different ways, to help create an impression of fog. They use language metaphorically in that they describe the fog as though it actually were a cat.

Read both poems carefully before answering the questions on them.

1 How does each poet use the image of a cat to give a particular impression of fog? Refer to particular words and phrases.

2 What are the main differences between the two images?

ACTIVITY 3

The next poem is full of imagery. Each word has been carefully selected to convey a particular picture of a city scene. The poem makes great use of personification. Personification means taking an inanimate object or abstract idea and making it seem like a person or animal. Read the poem several times and then answer the questions around it.

City Jungle

What does the word 'splinters' suggest?

Is this a friendly grin?

What different meaning can you find in these lines 5–6?

How can a gutter gargle?

What is the connection between the motorbike and the dustbins?

What words are used to suggest aggression?

Rain splinters town.

Lizard cars cruise by;
their radiators grin.

Thin headlights stare –
5   shop doorways keep
their mouths shut.

At the roadside
hunched houses cough.

Newspapers shuffle by,
10   hands in their pockets.
The gutter gargles.

A motorbike snarls;
Dustbins flinch.

Streetlights bare
15   their yellow teeth.
The motorway's
cat-black tongue
lashes across
the glistening back
20   of the tarmac night.

Pie Corbett

What kind of animal is a lizard?

In what way are the headlights threatening?

What image is created by the words 'hunched houses cough?'

What impression do you get of the newspapers?

What is the effect of the words 'bare' and 'yellow'?

117

ACTIVITY 4

Using the notes you have made to answer the questions on **City Jungle**, and other ideas you may have about the poem, write about the way the poet uses language to convey a particular impression of a city at night.

It might help you to organize your ideas in this order:

- overall impressions of the city as a threatening, polluted and dangerous place

- use of personification to create images

- animal imagery

- things you found particularly effective

- what you thought of the poem as a whole with particular attention to use of language.

Remember to refer to specific words or phrases to illustrate the points you make.

POINTS to remember

- Always try to write about the way the poet uses words to create a particular effect.

- Look closely at how individual words and phrases work within the poem as a whole.

Looking at form and structure

How can you tell at first glance that a piece of writing is a poem and not a prose passage? The answer lies in its shape and the way it is set out on the page. A poem looks different. Whether it follows a regular or irregular pattern, it is easy to distinguish it visually from prose.

The poetic form allows poets tremendous freedom to express their ideas in unusual or thought-provoking ways.

ACTIVITY 1

Look at the following poem and, before reading it, say what is unusual about its shape on the page.

Sea's cape

```
          I
          see
          gulls
          Icy
  5       gulls
          I see
          gulls screaming
          – Aye –
          I see seagulls
  10      screaming, see
          Ai YUY –
          scream

          … 'Ice CREAM'
          the seagulls
  15      seem to scream
          Hi Hi eee
          Ye – Icy seagulls!

          I see

          Gulls      see

  20      eyes

          cream
```

Michael Horovitz

Now read **Sea's cape** again carefully. It is essential that you read this poem aloud.

- In what ways is the poet experimenting with words and their sounds?

- What can you say about the use of dashes, pauses, lay-out, spacing, capital letters, italics and non-words?

- In what way does the shape of the poem relate to its sound?

- What do you think of this poem?

Form is an important feature of poetry as it can be used not only to reflect but also to emphasize meaning. Look at and read the following poem and then answer the questions in Activity 3.

Inventory

you left me

      nothing but nail

      parings orange peel

      empty nutshells half filled

5   ashtrays dirty

      cups with dregs of

      nightcaps an odd hair

      or two of yours on my

      comb gap toothed

10   bookshelves and a

      you shaped

      depression in my pillow.

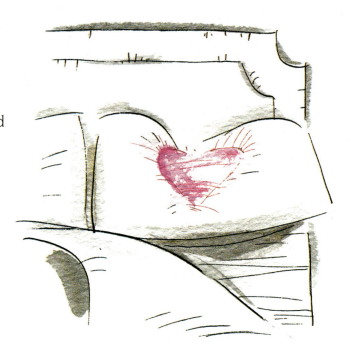

Liz Lochhead

- In what way does the poem's form relate to its title?

- How does the absence of punctuation affect the way that you read the poem?

- Why do you think the poet has presented her thoughts in this way?

- What difference would it make if the poem were written across the page like a piece of prose?
  You left me nothing but nail parings, orange peel, empty nutshells, half filled ashtrays, dirty cups with dregs of nightcaps, an odd hair or two of yours in my comb, gap toothed bookcase and a you shaped depression in my pillow.

Rhyme, rhythm and repetition

Poetry is intended to be read aloud and not simply seen on a page. It is the only way to hear the sounds of the words and the patterns of sound that are such an essential part of poetry. It is through listening to poetry and reading it aloud that we start to feel the rhythm of the words and to hear the impact of the rhymes and the repetition of particular words and phrases. Whatever rhythms, rhymes and repetitions the poet uses should be considered alongside the content and meaning of the poem.

Read the following poem aloud several times, perhaps trying out different ways of saying it, before answering the questions in Activity 4.

Nooligan

I'm a nooligan
dont give a toss
in our class
I'm the boss
5 (well, one of them)

I'm a nooligan
got a nard 'ead
step out of line
and youre dead
10 (well, bleedin)

I'm a nooligan
I spray me name
all over town
footballs me game
15 (well, watchin)

I'm a nooligan
violence is fun
gonna be a nassassin
or a hired gun
20 (well, a soldier)

Roger McGough

ACTIVITY 4

- What does each verse tell you about **Nooligan**?
- What do you learn about the 'nooligan' from the last line of each verse? What difference does it make to the rhythm?
- What use is made of rhyme within the poem?
- What is unusual about the words the poet uses?
- How does the poet use repetition to make the poem more effective?
- In what ways does the use of rhyme, rhythm and repetition in the poem make it easier to remember?

Bringing it all together

The poems you have looked at so far in this section reflect the link between what the poem is about, how the ideas are ordered within the poem and how those ideas are set out on the page.

ACTIVITY 5

Now read **The Identification** on the opposite page carefully and, once you feel comfortable that you know what it's about, try to answer the following questions.

1 How are the ideas organized? Think about:

- what each verse is about

- similarities between the start of the second, third and fourth verses

- the way the poet moves from doubt to certainty.

2 How does the poet create the impression that this is part of a conversation? Think about:

- what is said and how this is expressed

- the use of pauses

- the variation in sentence length

- the use of questions

- the irregular rhythm.

3 Find as many examples as you can of rhyme being used:

- at the ends of lines

- within lines.

4 What is the effect of the three short sentences at the end and the repetition of the word 'thats'?

POINTS *to remember*

- When writing about form you need to consider the way the words are set out on the page and the effect this has.

- You will become more aware of a poem's rhyme and rhythm if you read it aloud.

- Look carefully at the way the ideas are organised and the way the different parts of the poem relate to each other.

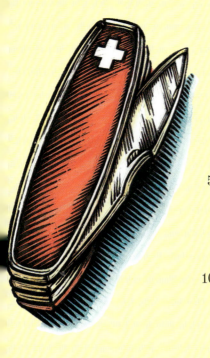

The Identification

So you think its Stephen?
Then I'd best make sure
Be on the safe side as it were.
Ah, theres been a mistake. The hair
5   you see, its black, now Stephens fair ...
Whats that? The explosion?
Of course, burnt black. Silly of me.
I should have known. Then lets get on.

The face, is that a face I ask?
10   that mask of charred wood
blistered, scarred could
that have been a child's face?
The sweater, where intact, looks
in fact all too familiar.
15   But one must be sure.

The scoutbelt. Yes thats his.
I recognise the studs he hammered in
not a week ago. At the age
when boys get clothes-conscious
20   now you know. Its almost
certainly Stephen. But one must
be sure. Remove all trace of doubt.
Pull out every splinter of hope.

Pockets. Empty the pockets.
25   Handkerchief? Could be any schoolboy's.
Dirty enough. Cigarettes?
Oh this can't be Stephen.
I don't allow him to smoke you see.
He wouldn't disobey me. Not his father.
30   But thats his penknife. Thats his alright.
And thats his key on the keyring
Gran gave him just the other night.
Then this must be him.

I think I know what happened
35   ...... about the cigarettes
No doubt he was minding them
for one of the older boys.
Yes thats it.
Thats him.
40   Thats our Stephen.

Roger McGough

Developing your own point of view

First of all, there is no one correct way of looking at a poem. A poem will mean different things to different people. You bring your own experience to every poem you read and this directly influences the effect it has on you. What you do need to do is to read each poem carefully and take time to understand it and appreciate the craft of the poet. The previous sections have tried to help you to do these things. Now you have the opportunity to use the skills you have acquired and to practise ways of comparing poems in a useful and constructive way.

ACTIVITY 1

The four poems that follow are all, in some way, about life and death.

Read them carefully, and preferably aloud, several times. While you are doing so:

● jot down any ideas that occur to you

● think about what each poet is saying about life and death

● identify the one that affects you most and decide why.

Long Distance

Though my mother was already two years dead
Dad kept her slippers warming by the gas,
put hot water bottles her side of the bed
and still went to renew her transport pass.

5 You couldn't just drop in. You had to phone.
He'd put you off an hour to give him time
to clear away her things and look alone
as though his still raw love were such a crime.

He couldn't risk my blight of disbelief
10 though sure that very soon he'd hear her key
scrape in the rusted lock and end his grief.
He *knew* she'd just popped out to get the tea.

I believe life ends with death, and that is all.
You haven't both gone shopping: just the same,
15 in my new black leather phone book there's your name
and the disconnected number I still call.

Tony Harrison

Poem

And if it snowed and snow covered the drive
he took a spade and tossed it to one side.
And always tucked his daughter up at night.
And slippered her the one time that she lied.

5   And every week he tipped up half his wage.
And what he didn't spend each week he saved.
And praised his wife for every meal she made.
And once, for laughing, punched her in the face.

And for his mum he hired a private nurse.
10   And every Sunday taxied her to church.
And he blubbed when she went from bad to worse.
And twice he lifted ten quid from her purse.

Here's how they rated him when they looked back:
sometimes he did this, sometimes he did that.

Simon Armitage

Do Not Go Gentle into That Good Night

Do not go gentle into that good night,
Old age should burn and rave at close of day;
Rage, rage against the dying of the light.

Though wise men at their end know dark is right,
5 Because their words had forked no lightning they
Do not go gentle into that good night.

Good men, the last wave by, crying how bright
Their frail deeds might have danced in a green bay,
Rage, rage against the dying of the light.

10 Wild men who caught and sang the sun in flight,
And learn, too late, they grieved it on its way,
Do not go gentle into that good night.

Grave men, near death, who see with blinding sight
Blind eyes could blaze like meteors and be gay,
15 Rage, rage against the dying of the light.

And you, my father, there on the sad height,
Curse, bless, me now with your fierce tears, I pray.
Do not go gentle into that good night.
Rage, rage against the dying of the light.

Dylan Thomas

Not Waving But Drowning

Nobody heard him, the dead man,
But still he lay moaning:
I was much further out than you thought
And not waving but drowning.

5 Poor chap, he always loved larking
And now he's dead
It must have been too cold for him his heart gave way,
They said.

Oh, no no no no, it was too cold always
10 (Still the dead one lay moaning)
I was much too far out all my life
And not waving but drowning.

Stevie Smith

ACTIVITY 2

Now that you have read the poems carefully and thought about them, you
need to start comparing the poems and developing your ideas in a more
structured way. It might be helpful to set your ideas down on a chart like the
one on page 128. You will need a big piece of paper. Looked at in this way, the
similarities and differences between the poems become much more obvious.

	Tony Harrison	*Simon Armitage*	*Dylan Thomas*	*Stevie Smith*
Meaning				
Argument				
Use of language				
Structure and form				
Rhyme and rhythm				
Your response				

ACTIVITY 3

Imagine you have been asked to give a talk to your class about two of these four poems.

- Which two would you choose? Why?
- What would you say about each of them? List your ideas in order of importance.
- What points of comparison or contrast would you make?

Make notes for the talk you would give.

POINTS to remember

- Use the skills you have acquired to help you understand and appreciate each new poem you read.

- Be prepared to state your own personal response to a poem and to explain this with reference to the text.

- Look for similarities and differences between poems and be prepared to compare their effectiveness.

GLOSSARY

Metaphor
An image in which the writer refers to one thing as *being* another thing. For example, in the poem **Toads** the poet describes work as a toad: *Why should I let the toad work/Squat on my life.*

Personification
An image in which an object or idea is made to appear to be a person and is given human characteristics. For example: *Newspapers shuffle by,/hands in their pockets.*

Simile
A direct comparison of one thing with another, often using the words 'as' or 'like'. For example: *Blind eyes could blaze like meteors.*

Tone
The mood of a poem, the tone of 'voice' the poem is written in. For example: humorous, angry, sarcastic.

Looking at texts from other cultures and traditions

First we need to establish what is meant, in this context, by the terms **cultures** and **traditions**.

Think about the following phrases and what they mean to you:

- youth culture
- urban culture
- rural culture
- a traditional Christmas
- a traditional wedding
- a traditional family

ACTIVITY 1

Talk about these terms with other people in your class.

- Do they mean the same things to them?
- Can you find reasons for any differences you may have?
- Would you expect someone from another country to have the same ideas as you? If not, why not?
- If you were to explain these terms to someone from another country what would you say about them?

ACTIVITY 2

Read the account of a traditional Hindu wedding on the opposite page. In what ways is it similar or different to your ideas of a traditional wedding?

Clearly traditions and customs are a part of the culture in which they arise. **Culture** refers to the vast range of ideas, beliefs, values and knowledge which underpin a given society. The term **traditions** refers more specifically to the customs handed down from one generation to another. Within one broad culture it is possible to have many different cultures and traditions.

All the poems in the first section of your English **Anthology** are written by poets considered to belong to the English literary tradition. The poems in *this* section stand outside this tradition. They may be written by someone from another culture or the subject matter may be obviously about another culture. It is the *otherness* of these poems that is their distinctive quality as a group. You should approach them in the same way as any other poem, although you should be aware of what they are telling you about other cultures and traditions at the same time.

The wedding ceremony usually lasts about an hour, but the celebrations often go on for several days. The wedding takes place either in a temple or the bride's home. The
5 bride wears special eye make-up, and a dye is used to make patterns on her hands and feet. She wears a new red and gold sari, and lots of gold jewellery. Preparing the bride for the ceremony takes several
10 hours. Both the bride and groom wear garlands of flowers.

The first part of the wedding is when the bride's father welcomes the bridegroom. The bridegroom sits under a special
15 canopy, which is a decorated covering. He is given small presents which are symbols of happiness and a good life. Then the bride arrives, usually wearing a veil so that her face cannot be seen. She removes this
20 during the ceremony. The couple sit in front of a special fire. Their right hands are tied together and holy water is sprinkled on them when the bride's father 'gives' her to the bridegroom. There are prayers and
25 offerings of rice.

The most important part of the ceremony is when the bride and groom take seven steps towards the fire. At each step they stop and make promises to each other.
30 While they do this, they are joined by a piece of cloth. It is hung loosely round the bridegroom's neck, and tied to the bride's sari. This is a symbol that they are being joined as husband and wife. Once they
35 have taken the steps together, they are married. There are more prayers and readings, and flower petals are thrown before the guests give their wedding presents. Then everyone shares a meal.

ACTIVITY 3

Read the four poems on pages 132–135 carefully, preferably aloud, several times. The prompts will help you think about different aspects of the poems. The question at the end of each poem is intended as a starting point for discussion about meaning and form.

Grace Nichols was born in Guyana and came to Britain in 1977. She wrote **Island Man** *'for a Caribbean island man in London who still wakes up to the sound of the sea'.*

Island Man

Morning
and island man wakes up
to the sound of blue surf
in his head
5   the steady breaking and wombing

wild seabirds
and fishermen pushing out to sea
the sun surfacing defiantly

from the east
10   of his small emerald island
he always comes back   groggily groggily

Comes back to sands
of a grey metallic soar
         to surge of wheels
15   to dull North Circular roar

muffling muffling
his crumpled pillow waves
island man heaves himself

Another London day

Grace Nichols

What is being described in lines 1–5?

How would you describe the tone of the first three verses?

What change occurs here? Which words emphasize that change?

Is the poem about dream and reality?

Discussion: **How does the poet use sound and rhythm to reflect meaning?**

Decorated for a Kiss

I come to her house for love with a basket of red petals.
Men-friend tell me what a fool to go to the girl
Come, man, come fish shark, strong white shark,
At midnight come fish golden snapper along the warm black rocks.
5 But I decide my mind and come to her for love.
Her dress is patterned with blue dragon-flies
She has put a red bead in each ear
Green lizards run in her eyes
Her body has the scent of sun-dried khus-khus grass
10 The sweet fibres she has put between the linen since midday
She has washed her mouth with milk
She has rubbed her lips with bay leaves
She has made her limbs clean with water from a green calabash
Now she offers me a few plums and palm-wine from a gourd of
15   scarlet leather.

Ian McDonald

What is unusual about the word order here? What different creatures does the poet refer to and for what effect?

What customs are associated with love?

Discussion: **In what ways do you think this poem belongs to another culture?**

Palm-Tree

Palm-tree:	single-legged giant,
	topping the other trees,
	peering at the firmament –
It longs	to pierce the black cloud-ceiling
5	and fly away, away,
	if only it had wings.
The tree	seems to express its wish
	in the tossing of its head:
	its fronds heave and swish –
10 It thinks,	Maybe my leaves are feathers,
	and nothing stops me now
	from rising on their flutter.
All day	the fronds on the windblown tree
	soar and flap and shudder
15	as though it thinks it can fly,
As though	it wanders in the skies,
	travelling who knows where,
	wheeling past the stars –
And then	as soon as the wind dies down,
20	the fronds subside, subside:
	the mind of the tree returns
To earth,	recalls that earth is its mother
	and then it likes once more
	its earthly corner.

Rabindranath Tagore

How is the palm tree described?

What is the effect of this description?

How is the tree made to seem human?

How does the poet create a sense of freedom?

What happens to the tree when the wind dies?

What might the tree represent?

Discussion: **What is unusual about the form of this poem and why do you think the poet has chosen it?**

Trumpet Player

The Negro
With the trumpet at his lips
Has dark moons of weariness
Beneath his eyes
5 Where the smoldering memory
Of slave ships
Blazed to the crack of whips
About his thighs.

The Negro
10 With the trumpet at his lips
Has a head of vibrant hair
Tamed down,
Patent-leathered now
Until it gleams
15 Like jet –
Were jet a crown.

The music
From the trumpet at his lips
Is honey
20 Mixed with liquid fire.
The rhythm
From the trumpet at his lips
Is ecstasy
Distilled from old desire –

25 Desire
That is longing for the moon
Where the moonlight's but a spotlight
In his eyes,
Desire
30 That is longing for the sea
Where the sea's a bar-glass
Sucker size.

Which words conjure up images of fire? How is the past linked to the present?

What do the words 'Tamed down' suggest?

Why is the music described in this way?

The Negro
With the trumpet at his lips
35 Whose jacket
Has a *fine* one-button roll,
Does not know
Upon what riff the music slips
Its hypodermic needle
40 To his soul –

But softly
As the tune comes from his throat
Trouble
Mellows to a golden note.

Langston Hughes

What effect does the music have on the Negro?

Discussion: **How effective is this as a description of a person?**

ACTIVITY 4

Now that you have spent some time reading and thinking about these poems you can start expressing some of your ideas in writing. Explore these five main areas with reference to each poem:

- the meaning and the way the ideas are organized and developed

- how the words are set out on the page and the reasons for this particular form

- how the words are used individually, and in combination with others, to create a particular effect

- your own response to the poem, giving reasons.

- what is revealed about other cultures and traditions.

ACTIVITY 5

Using your notes to Activity 4 to help you, write about **two** of the poems from this selection, explaining what you found of interest in their content, form and use of language.

POINTS to remember

- These poems should be approached in the same way as any others in terms of understanding and appreciation.

- An additional factor to be aware of is what they reveal of **other** cultures and traditions.

Exam Practice – Foundation Tier

PAPER 2 SECTION A

- Answer *two* questions in this section, *one* from Part 1 (*Poets*) and *one* from Part 2 (*Poems from Other Cultures and Traditions*).
- Spend *about one hour* on this section.

PART 1: POETS

In the examination the questions in this part will be based on the poets who feature in the first part of your **NEAB Anthology**. These sample questions are based on the four poems in the unit 'Developing your own point of view' in this book.*

Answer *one* of the following questions.

Either

Write about *two* of the poems which interested you. Include comments on the following:

- the ideas and attitudes
- how the poems are set out
- how particular words and phrases bring out the ideas
- your personal response to the poems.

Or

What have you learnt about grief and/or bereavement from reading **Long Distance** and **Do Not Go Gentle into That Good Night**? You should consider:

- what the poems are about
- how the ideas are presented
- similarities/differences

PART 2: POEMS FROM OTHER CULTURES AND TRADITIONS

In the examination the questions in this part will be based on the poems in the 'Other Cultures and Traditions' section of your **NEAB Anthology**. These sample questions are based on the four poems in the unit 'Looking at texts from other cultures and traditions' in this book.*

Answer *one* of the following questions.

Either

Choose *two* poems in which a person is described. Write about how the poets have used words and details to:

- make the people interesting
- tell you about their particular culture.

Or

Which *two* poems do you consider to be most interesting? Explain your choice by writing about:

- ideas and attitudes
- the way the ideas are set out
- the words used
- what is revealed of other cultures.

* Note: you will find exam practice questions covering the *specific* poems in your **Anthology** in *Working with the English Anthology* from Heinemann.

Exam Practice – Higher Tier

PAPER 2 SECTION A

- Answer *two* questions in this section, *one* from Part 1 (*Poets*) and *one* from Part 2 (*Poems from Other Cultures and Traditions*).
- Spend *about one hour* on this section.

PART 1: POETS

In the examination the questions in this part will be based on the poets who feature in the first part of your **NEAB Anthology**. These sample questions are based on the four poems in the unit '**Developing your own point of view**' in this book.*

Answer *one* of the following questions.

Either

Write about how Dylan Thomas and *one* other poet present ideas on both life and death in their poems. You should consider:

- the ideas
- the ways these are presented
- the poets' viewpoints.

Or

All these poems express strong feelings but in different ways. Which *two* poems do you consider to be most effective? Explain your choice by writing about:

- ideas and feelings
- language
- form
- your personal response.

PART 2: POEMS FROM OTHER CULTURES AND TRADITIONS

In the examination the questions in this part will be based on the poems in the 'Other Cultures and Traditions' section of your **NEAB Anthology**. These sample questions are based on the four poems in the unit '**Looking at texts from other cultures and traditions**' in this book.*

Answer *one* of the following questions.

Either

Write about the importance of form and language in **Island Man** and **Palm-Tree**.

Or

Write about the extent to which the influence of other cultures and traditions is evident in *two* of the poems in this selection. You should think about:

- subject matter
- structure
- form
- use of language.

* Note: you will find exam practice questions covering the *specific* poems in your
Anthology in *Working with the English Anthology* from Heinemann.

Working with your Anthology

The examiner comments ...

Now you have worked through the sections on poetry you need to think how you can apply what you have learnt to the poems in your **Anthology**. During your course you will be studying at least one of the poets from the English literary tradition and the poems from the Other Cultures and Traditions section. In your examination you will be asked to answer *one* question on each.

Use the Assessment Objectives to approach the poem

Understanding the text
- Ask yourself questions about the meaning of the poem: Who? What? Where? When? Why? How?
- Are there other meanings buried beneath the surface?
- Are there any significant symbols or images? How are they used? What do they mean?
- What is the mood or tone of the poem?

Referring to the text
- Which words, phrases or lines have particular significance?
- Are there any words or phrases that are repeated for deliberate effect?
- How might you use these when writing about the poem?

Following an argument
- Is a particular argument or viewpoint developed in the poem?
- Can you trace its different stages?
- What are your opinions on the viewpoint expressed in the poem?

Looking at language
- How does the writer use words to create particular images or to convey specific ideas or moods?
- What phrases can you select to exemplify this?
- How effective are these images?

Looking at form and structure
- What can you say about the way the words are set out on the page?
- Is rhyme used? If so, what is its effect?
- Is the rhythm regular or irregular? What is its effect?
- How are the ideas organized?

Develop your own point of view

- What did you think of the poems when you first read them?

- How have your views changed after looking at them more closely?

- Which ones appeal to you most? What qualities made you prefer them?

All these questions are relevant to the poems in *both* sections.

When looking at the poems from 'Other Cultures and Traditions' you need also to think about the ways in which they are different from the English literary tradition.

Compare poems

It is likely that you will also be asked to make comparisons between different poems – to point out the similarities and/or differences between them. You might decide to write about each poem separately and then summarize the similarities and differences between them at the end. Alternatively you could look at one particular aspect of the poems at a time. For example, you might look at the significance of form and structure in each of the poems before moving on to examine the use of language.

Annotate your Anthology

The rules about annotation of the **Anthology** are very clearly laid down in the NEAB syllabus and you must take care to follow these:

Annotation means brief hand-written marginal notes, underlinings, highlightings and vertical lines in the margin. Additional notes on loose, interleaved sheets of paper and/or prepared answers are not *permitted.*

You will probably find it most helpful to make all your notes on the poems in a separate notebook or file at first and only start to annotate your **Anthology** when specifically preparing for the examination or revising.

Time your answers

You have 1 hour for Section A of this paper. In that time you must answer *one* question on your chosen poet and *one* question on the poems from 'Other Cultures and Traditions'. Once you take away reading and selection time this gives you about 25 minutes writing time for each answer, so you will need to be very selective in the information you include, making sure you target the points raised in the question. Practise writing answers in timed conditions.

Section B

In your exam you will be given a choice of writing tasks which require you to inform, explain or describe. Some of these tasks will be linked to themes in the **Anthology** poems studied for Section A.

Your examiner will be looking for the same range of writing skills as were tested in Paper 1 Section B. Here is a quick reminder of those skills.

Mechanics of writing:

- your handwriting should be legible and the presentation of your work should be neat and clear
- words should be spelt correctly
- your writing should be correctly punctuated
- you are expected to organize your ideas in sentences and paragraphs and to communicate them clearly.

Effectiveness of writing:

- your vocabulary should be varied and appropriate, demonstrating a knowledge and understanding of a range of words
- your sentences should be correctly structured and varied
- you should show an awareness of both audience and purpose and the ability to adapt your writing style to suit these.

How this section helps

Whilst the skills you are being tested on are the same, the ways in which you are asked to demonstrate them are different. The emphasis in this section is on the ability to write in a more *personal and/or descriptive* way. In the next few pages we look at examples of the different types of writing you will be asked to do and the ways you should use and improve the skills you have, and develop new skills. For the purpose of study and practice here the three areas of focus (inform, explain and describe) are dealt with separately, but in the exam they will often be combined. The practice questions at the end of this section will show you how this works.

Writing to inform

When you are writing to inform your aim is to tell the reader about something or someone. It may be that you have been asked to write about a significant incident or person in your life, or about a particular occasion such as a school outing or a time when you made a serious mistake. It is important to make the distinction between this kind of writing, based on personal experience, and story-writing.

In the following extract Maya Angelou writes about her brother Bailey and makes clear his importance to her:

Bailey was the greatest person in my world. And the fact that he was my brother, my only brother, and I had no sisters to share him with, was such good fortune that it made me want to live a Christian life just to show God that I was
5 grateful. Where I was big, elbowy and grating, he was small, graceful and smooth. When I was described by our playmates as being shit color, he was lauded for his velvet-black skin. His hair fell down in black curls, and my head was covered with black steel wool. And yet he loved me.

10 When our elders said unkind things about my features (my family was handsome to a point of pain for me), Bailey would wink at me from across the room, and I knew that it was a matter of time before he would take revenge. He would allow the old ladies to finish wondering how on
15 earth I came about, then he would ask, in a voice like cooling bacon grease, "Oh Mizeriz Coleman, how is your son? I saw him the other day and he looked sick enough to die."

Aghast, the ladies would ask, "Die? From what? He ain't sick."

20 And in a voice oilier than the one before, he'd answer with a straight face, "From the Uglies."

I would hold my laugh, bite my tongue, grit my teeth and very seriously erase even the touch of a smile from my face. Later, behind the house by the black-walnut tree, we'd
25 laugh and laugh and howl.

Bailey could count on very few punishments for his consistently outrageous behavior, for he was the pride of the Henderson/Johnson family.

His movements, as he was later to describe those of an acquaintance, were activated with oiled precision. He was also able to find more hours in the day than I thought existed. He finished chores, homework, read more books than I and played the group games on the side of the hill with the best of them. He could even pray out loud in church, and was apt at stealing pickles from the barrel that sat under the fruit counter and Uncle Willie's nose. 35

Once when the Store was full of lunchtime customers, he dipped the strainer, which we also used to sift weevils from meal and flour, into the barrel and fished for two fat pickles. He caught them and hooked the strainer onto the side of the barrel where they dripped until he was ready for them. When the last school 40 bell rang, he picked the nearly dry pickles out of the strainer, jammed them into his pockets and threw the strainer behind the oranges. We ran out of the Store. It was summer and his pants were short, so the pickle juice made clean streams down his ashy 45 legs, and he jumped with his pockets full of loot and his eyes laughing a "How about that?" He smelled like a vinegar barrel or a sour angel.

After our early chores were done, while Uncle Willie or Momma minded the Store, we were free to 50 play the children's games as long as we stayed within yelling distance. Playing hide-and-seek, his voice was easily identified, singing, "Last night, night before, twenty-four robbers at my door. Who all is hid? Ask me to let them in, hit 'em in the head with a rolling 55 pin. Who all is hid?" In follow the leader, naturally he was the one who created the most daring and inter-esting things to do. And when he was on the tail of the pop the whip, he would twirl off the end like a top, spinning, falling, laughing, finally stopping just 60 before my heart beat its last, and then he was back in the game, still laughing.

Of all the needs (there are none imaginary) a lonely child has, the one that must be satisfied, if there is going to be hope and a hope of wholeness, 65 is the unshaking need for an unshakable God. My pretty Black brother was my Kingdom Come.

I Know Why the Caged Bird Sings
by Maya Angelou

ACTIVITY 1

In the extract on pages 142–3 Maya Angelou tells her reader many different things about her brother.

In the first paragraph she describes what he looks like in comparison to herself. By giving a specific example of his behaviour (lines 10 to 21) she then shows how he would defend her. Some direct speech gives the reader a flavour of how he talks.

Summarize briefly what you learn about Bailey from reading:

● lines 1 to 9

● lines 10 to 21

● lines 26 to 35

● lines 36 to 48

● lines 49 to 62.

ACTIVITY 2

Such informative descriptions help to make this account both lively and interesting. Of course it is not just what she says about her brother that is important. This is personal writing and reveals much about the writer herself. In the first paragraph, for example, the reader learns not only of the writer's belief in God but also of her own lack of self-confidence in her appearance.

Read through the passage again and make notes on any other things you learn about Maya Angelou.

ACTIVITY 3

The effectiveness of a piece of writing depends largely on the way the writer expresses ideas. Maya Angelou's language is filled with imagery which gives it vitality and interest. Look at these phrases – what is the effect of each image?

● my head was covered with black steel wool

● in a voice like cooling bacon grease

● His movements … were activated with oiled precision.

● He smelled like a vinegar barrel or a sour angel.

● he would twirl off the end like a top, spinning, falling, laughing

● My pretty Black brother was my Kingdom Come.

Can you find some more?

POINTS to remember

● The effectiveness of your writing is dependent on **what** you say and **how** you say it.

● There are many different ways of structuring your writing to make it more interesting.

● Ideas should be planned carefully before you start to write.

Writing your own

Choose a relative of yours to write about. Your aim is to tell your reader about him or her. Use the structure below to help you.

Getting your ideas together

First jot down ideas in response to the following questions:

- what does s/he look like?
- how does s/he talk?
- where does s/he live?
- what does s/he do?
- has s/he any distinctive features?
- how does s/he behave?

Now make brief notes on any particular incidents which would help to illustrate the kind of person s/he is. Try to look at different aspects of personality and interests.

Finally, think about your own feelings towards this person. What words would you use to describe these feelings?

Organizing your ideas

Now that you have generated some ideas you are ready to start organizing them. You could follow a similar structure to that used by Maya Angelou but there are many other alternatives. Here are just a few possibilities for you to consider:

- Time based: show how the person has changed and developed over a number of years. This might be a useful way to write about a younger brother or sister.

- Photograph: focus on the person at a particular time and place. This structure could work well if you are writing about someone who is now dead, perhaps a grandparent.

- Contrast: write about the person in two or more very different situations e.g. after a hard day's work and on holiday. This is one way of showing the different roles of a person, such as a parent.

Remember, these are only some of the options – there are many other ways of structuring your writing.

Before starting to write, think carefully about:

- the impression you want to give your reader. What tone(s) should you adopt in your writing to best achieve this effect, e.g. humorous, serious, affectionate?

- the ways you can best use language to convey your ideas about this person to your reader. What images would be appropriate? Should direct speech be included?

- your introduction and your ending. Look back at the Maya Angelou passage and consider the close connection between 'Bailey was the greatest person in my world' and 'My pretty Black brother was my Kingdom Come'.

Your plan

Once you have considered all the options carefully you need to put all your ideas into a plan. You wouldn't set out on a journey without first working out how to get to your destination. The same is true of writing. You need to work out which details you are going to include and the order in which they are going to appear.

Your plan might look something like this:

My Baby Brother!

start
- First sentence: Here he is, invading my space again, asking all sorts of irritating questions and embarrassing me in front of my friends.
- Para. 1 — as he is now at 10 years — what he looks like — the way he behaves
- Para. 2 — remembering him as a new-born baby — what he was like then — my feelings for him

middle
- Para. 3 — the time he fell in the fish pond when he was 3
- Para. 4 — his first day at school
- Para. 5 — when I took him for the bike ride to Aunt Jane's
- Para. 6 — the tricks he's played on me and other members of the family

end
- Para. 7 — now he's about to start secondary school — the things that might happen to him
- Last sentence: No matter what the future holds, or how big he grows, he will always be my 'baby' brother.

Once you have planned your structure you are ready to start writing. Remember, you will be assessed on the *way* that you write about the given subject so your aim should be to make your writing as interesting and effective as you can.

Writing to explain

When you explain you give reasons. If a teacher asks you at school why you have done something, he or she is not asking for a report on what you have done but for an explanation as to *why* you have done it. You might also be asked to explain *how* something is done or *what* the effect of something might be.

In the following passage a teenager explains how he developed an interest in running. Read it carefully and then answer the questions in Activity 1.

A little less than a year ago I was a tubby 14-year-old, feeding on chips and chocolate bars. My idea of exercise was changing TV channels by remote control. Now I am a lean
5 15-year-old who eats baked potatoes and natural crunch bars, with a regular training schedule.

One day I found myself glued to the 'box' watching an international athletics meeting at Gateshead. It looked so much fun. All those
10 strong athletes coasting around a 400-metre track at high speed. So, I thought I would have a go at it. The next day was warm and sunny with just a little light breeze. I donned my tracksuit bottoms, school athletics vest and best trainers,
15 and I set off on a one-mile run. It was not as bad as I thought it was going to be and it took me just under eight minutes.

The next day was a different matter. I was as stiff as a board and I could hardly kneel down!
20 But I went out again. And again and again. The stiffness went away and I did nothing but improve. After about two weeks I started doing two miles a day. Then 2.5 miles and 3 miles, gradually building up my stamina.
25 I decided to cut out all that excess sugar and fat from my diet. It didn't feel like 'slimming' because I wasn't eating less, just eating differently. I became a 'health fooder'. Porridge oats for breakfast, wholemeal bread in my lunch-box,
30 chilli beans for dinner. It all seemed very filling! I drank just as much milk as before, only now it was skimmed milk. And I ate fresh fruit and

Shows contrast between past and present

Explains why and how he started to run

Extends focus to look at diet

yoghurt instead of cakes and puddings. Already I was feeling fitter and looking better.

35   Three and a half months after I started training I had a talk with one of my dad's friends who was a running coach. He told me that my running was lacking two factors: SPEED and STRENGTH. Also, the fact that I didn't have any rest days wasn't good for me or my running.
40   He gave me a training programme which I have basically followed ever since.

   My schedule has changed a lot since the early days when every day was a 2.5 mile run. The times have changed a lot too. I would have taken
45   about 17 minutes to get round that 2.5 mile circuit then. Now it would take me under 12.30.

   Just after Christmas, to strengthen my arms and legs, and for more sprinting power, I took up

Focuses on significant turning point

Moves to present to emphasize progress

50 light weight-training using dumb-bells. I've read lots of articles which claim that weight-training is bad for your body if your body is still growing. But I think that if you are pretty fit, and do not use too heavy weights, it will help your running a
55 lot. I never lift anything over 20 kgs at any one time. Then, at half-term I got a weight-bench and bar-bell. The weight-bench has leg-extension attachments, and the use of these in my training has really put muscles onto my legs.

60 My running has had its good and bad days, sad and funny days. There was the day I ran off the road onto the beach to find that the tide had come in. It was a very high tide. I had to run knee-deep in water for over two miles! I remem-
65 ber one particularly bad day when I did a cross-country run in deep snow and I seemed to be more on my bum than on my feet. That experience taught me not to run in deep snow again.

The obsession called 'NOT MISSING
70 TRAINING' can be dangerous! Sad days are when you get sick or injured and cannot run. This winter I had a chest cold which stopped my running for a whole week! But every runner has good days. These are the days when everything
75 goes right, you feel great, and you set a personal best: like last Wednesday, when I ran 38.30 for my five-mile training run in the rain.

It's always said that it's helpful to have some target to attain. So, I hope to see you at the
80 Olympics!

MATTHEW BRIDGEMAN

Extends focus to explain how progress was made

Gives examples of unfortunate experiences

Highlights main achievement

Looks to the future

ACTIVITY 1

One difficulty students sometimes have in this kind of writing is in developing their ideas in sufficient detail. The notes in italics in the margin highlight the key points of Matthew Bridgeman's developing interest in running.

- What are your first impressions of this passage? Did you find it interesting to read?
- Are there areas that could have been developed further and others that would have been better left out? Say which these are and why.
- What do you learn about Matthew himself from reading this passage?

POINTS to remember

- Try to develop your ideas in detail before writing by asking yourself a series of questions.
- Organize your ideas carefully into the most appropriate and effective order.
- Don't rely too heavily on factual detail at the expense of interesting and lively writing.

Writing your own

ACTIVITY 2

Write about an interest that you have, explaining how that interest has developed and its importance to you. Use the structure below to help you.

Getting your ideas together

It may be that a particular interest springs to mind straight away but often it is not that straightforward. Here are some suggestions for the kind of thing you could write about:

cricket	fashion	music	art	computer games
a school subject	animals	foreign travel	dancing	my football club
a hobby	snooker	reading	drama	

Once you have decided on your subject you need to generate some ideas. Make brief notes in answer to the following questions:

- When and how did you first become interested in this?
- What does the interest involve?
- How much time do you give to it?
- What do you enjoy about it?

- Are there any drawbacks?
- Have you made new friends through it?
- Can you think of any funny or odd things that have happened because of it?
- Will your interest have any influence on your future?

Once you have collected some ideas together you are ready to start planning your writing. You need to decide what you are going to include and in what order you are going to write it. It might help you to organize your ideas around sub-headings which can later be replaced with paragraphing.

e.g. Football
When I first became interested   Details about the game
Me as a player   My favourite Football Club
A typical home match   Away games

Make your own sub-headings for your chosen subject. Under each sub-heading write brief notes on the details you would include, and then arrange your sub-headings into the most appropriate order.

Now you are ready to write. Remember that this is a piece of *personal* writing and should tell the reader things about you as well as your interest.

Writing to describe

Perhaps the best way to improve your own skills in descriptive writing is to look at descriptions written by other writers and assess the qualities that make them effective.

In the extract below Roald Dahl describes his first sighting of Dar es Salaam, in Tanzania, Africa. Read the description carefully and then answer the questions below.

DAR ES SALAAM

WHEN I WOKE UP the next morning the ship's engines had stopped. I jumped out of my bunk and peered through the port-hole. This was my first glimpse of Dar es Salaam and I have never
5 forgotten it. We were anchored out in the middle of a vast rippling blue-black lagoon and all around the rim of the lagoon there were pale-yellow sandy beaches, almost white, and breakers were running up on to the sand, and coconut palms
10 with their little green leafy hats were growing on the beaches, and there were casuarina trees, immensely tall and breathtakingly beautiful with their delicate grey-green foliage. And then behind the casuarinas was what seemed to me like a
15 jungle, a great tangle of tremendous dark-green

42

trees that were full of shadows and almost certainly teeming, so I told myself, with rhinos and lions and all manner of vicious beasts. Over to one side lay the tiny town of Dar es Salaam, the houses white and yellow and pink, and among the houses 20
I could see a narrow church steeple and a domed mosque and along the waterfront there was a line of acacia trees splashed with scarlet flowers. A fleet of canoes was rowing out to take us ashore and the black-skinned rowers were chanting 25
weird songs in time with their rowing.
   The whole of that amazing tropical scene through the port-hole has been photographed on my mind ever since. To me it was all wonderful, beautiful and exciting. And so it remained for the 30
rest of my time in Tanganyika. I loved it all. There were no furled umbrellas, no bowler hats, no sombre grey suits and I never once had to get on a train or a bus.

43

GOING SOLO BY ROALD DAHL

ACTIVITY 1

In what order does Dahl reveal the detail of what he sees? How does this help to create the impression of a 'first glimpse'?

- What is the effect of the very long fourth sentence (lines 5–13)?
- How does Dahl use colour to make his description more vivid?
- Comment on the effectiveness of the words underlined:

    casuarina trees, underlined immensely tall and breathtakingly beautiful
    coconut palms with their little green leafy hats
    a great tangle of tremendous dark-green trees
    a line of acacia trees splashed with scarlet flowers.

In the extract from **Going Solo** Dahl presents the details of his first glimpse of Dar es Salaam in quick succession so that the reader can see it in the same way that he did. The speed with which he relates these details helps to create the feelings of excitement and enthusiasm which he experienced at the time. Creation of mood and atmosphere is an important element of descriptive writing.

The extract below is taken from the opening of a famous book by John Steinbeck. Read it carefully before answering the questions in Activity 2. It may help you to read the passage aloud.

Salinas River

A few miles south of Soledad, the Salinas River drops in close to the hill-side bank and runs deep and green. The water is warm too, for it has slipped twinkling over the yellow sands in the sunlight before reaching the narrow pool. On one side of
5 the river the golden foot-hill slopes curve up to the strong and rocky Gabilan mountains, but on the valley side the water is lined with trees – willows fresh and green with every spring, carrying in their lower leaf-junctures the debris of the winter's flooding; and sycamores with mottled, white, recumbent
10 limbs and branches that arch over the pool. On the sandy bank under the trees the leaves lie deep and so crisp that a lizard makes a great skittering if he runs among them. Rabbits come out of the brush to sit on the sand in the evening, and the damp flats are covered with the night tracks of 'coons, and
15 with the spread pads of dogs from the ranches, and with the split-wedge tracks of deer that come to drink in the dark.
There is a path through the willows and among the sycamores, a path beaten hard by boys coming down from the highway in the evening to jungle-up near water. In front of the
20 low horizontal limb of a giant sycamore there is an ash pile made by many fires; the limb is worn smooth by men who have sat on it.

Of Mice and Men by John Steinbeck

The previous two extracts have described outdoor, natural scenes. In the following passage a very different kind of place is described. Read the extract carefully and then answer the questions in Activity 3.

It was here that a few amusements were situated. Most of them were closed at this time of year, but I liked to wander past the canvas shrouded dodgem cars and shuttered gift stalls. I enjoyed the tawdriness of it all, the blank lights and peeling
5   paint. There was an open air swimming pool, drained for the winter, and sand and silt had been washed over the rim by the storm tides. Near to this was a cafe and one amusement centre, called Gala Land, both of which remained open.

I could not keep away from Gala Land. It had a particular
10 smell which drew me down the steep flight of concrete steps to the pay desk below. It was built underground in a sort of valley between two outcrops of rock, over which was a ribbed glass roof, like those Victorian railway stations and conservatories. The walls were covered in greenish moss and
15 the whole place had a close, damp, musty smell and although it was lit from end to end with neon and fluorescent lights, everything looked somehow dark, furtive and gone to seed. Some of the booths were closed down here, too, and those which kept open must have lost money, except perhaps on the
20 few days when parties of trippers came from inland, in the teeth of the weather, and dived for shelter to the underground fun palace. Then, for a few hours, the fruit and try-your-strength and fortune card machines whirred, loud cracks echoed from the rifle ranges, hurdygurdy music sounded out,
25 there was a show of gaiety. For the rest of the time the place was mainly patronised by a few unemployed men and teenager boys, who chewed gum and fired endless rounds of blank ammunition at the bobbing rows of duck targets, and by older school children after four o'clock. At the far end was a roller
30 skating rink which drew a good crowd on Saturday afternoons.

I liked the sad, shabby place, I liked its atmosphere. Occasionally I put a coin into a fruit machine or watched "What the Butler Saw". There was a more gruesome peep-show, too, in which one could watch a condemned man being
35 led onto a platform, hooded and noosed and the dropped snap, down through a trapdoor to death. I watched this so often, that, long after I had left the town, this scene featured in my nightmares, I smelled the brackish, underground smell.

MR PROUDHAM AND MR SLEIGHT BY SUSAN HILL

ACTIVITY 3

Writers can use some or all of the five senses (sight, hearing, taste, smell and touch) in order to create an effective description. How does Susan Hill describe the smell of the Amusement Arcade?

Comment on the effect of the words underlined:

- the canvas <u>shrouded</u> dodgem cars
- the <u>blank</u> lights and <u>peeling</u> paint
- everything looked somehow <u>dark, furtive and gone to seed</u>
- there was <u>a show of</u> gaiety
- and fired <u>endless rounds</u> of blank ammunition.

What does the description of the 'gruesome peep-show' add to the reader's impression of this place?

POINTS to remember

- When reading pay close attention to how other writers describe people, places and events.
- Mood and atmosphere are important elements of descriptive writing.
- Linking ideas to the five senses (sight, hearing, taste, smell and touch) will help you to build up descriptive detail.

Writing your own

When you are writing a description you are trying to get across to your reader what a particular place, person, animal, object or feeling is or was like. It will help if you can generate as many ideas as you can in the early thinking stages – then you can select from these when you start to write.

One way of doing this is by using your five senses: sight, hearing, taste, smell and touch.

Task: Imagine you are sitting on a bench in a park on a summer's day.

Describe the scene before you. First, jot down as many ideas as you can in answer to the following questions:

- What do you see?
- What do you hear?
- Can you taste anything?
- What can you smell?
- What can you feel?

Now try to develop your ideas a little further. Look at the things listed under what you can see. Perhaps you've included children playing, people walking or someone sunbathing. Start to build up a pool of descriptive words or phrases for each thing you have listed, e.g. children playing: excitedly, energetically, furiously, like bees buzzing, like prisoners on their first day of freedom.

Further ideas may come from this, e.g. one little boy in tattered T-shirt and shorts starts to cry helplessly. Spend about five minutes generating ideas and words in this way.

Once you have got lots of ideas and the scene is clear in your mind you are ready to start organizing your writing. There are many different ways of doing this. Basically you need to give your writing some point of focus, something that links the ideas together. Here are some suggestions for writing about the park:

- follow one person, perhaps a little brother or sister, as they move around the park
- you are waiting for someone – record your impressions as the minutes tick by
- first impressions followed by more precise observations of particular things of interest
- match mood changes to impressions: perhaps you are depressed when you first sit down and gradually you start to feel more cheerful.

Once you have decided on a point of focus you are ready to select appropriate material from your notes, to arrange it into a suitable order and to start writing.

Constantly remind yourself as you are writing that your reader cannot see what is in your mind and it is up to you to choose the best words to paint your picture as clearly as you can.

Now go through this process again to describe the same park at dusk on a winter's day.

Exam Practice

Foundation Tier

- Answer *one* question in this section.
- You should spend *about one hour* on this section.

1   Write about a time when you wanted to, or actually did, leave home and describe your feelings at the time.

2   A student from another area is coming to stay with you. Write a letter telling him or her about your home and local area, explaining what you plan to do during the visit.

3   Many people think it's important to have a room of their own to escape to. Describe the room that you would like to have, making clear the reasons for your choice.

Higher Tier

- Answer *one* question in this section.
- You should spend *about one hour* on this section.

1   Many writers recall significant events in their lives and explain how these have affected them. Write about the most significant events in your life, showing how they have affected you.

2   Many people have strongly held views on a range of topics such as cruelty to animals, dangerous sports or environmental issues. Write about a topic which arouses strong feelings in you. Make your feelings and the reasons for them clear to your reader.

3   A room can often reflect its owner's personality. Write about a room which you think does this and explain your choice.

The examiner comments ...

This section is testing you on your ability to inform, explain or describe. It is unlikely that any one task would ask you to do all three types of writing but it may well ask you to do two of them. You need to think about the tasks in terms of the kinds of writing you are expected to produce. Here is a breakdown of the types of writing you are being asked to do on the practice papers:

Foundation Tier

1 Inform and Describe

2 Inform and Explain

3 Describe and Explain

Higher Tier

1 Inform and Explain

2 Inform and Explain

3 Describe and Explain

Make sure, before selecting your task, that you have plenty to write about the given subject. There is no point starting on a task, spending ten minutes trying to generate ideas and then deciding you should have made a different choice.

Once you have made your selection use the skills you have developed in the previous chapters to help you generate and plan your ideas. Remember that this is an important stage in the writing process and worth spending time on.

As you are writing be aware of the need to write legibly, to use paragraphing and to achieve a good level of technical accuracy in both spelling and punctuation. Most importantly you should aim to express your ideas as clearly, effectively and interestingly as you can. Look at the following examples:

a) In the corner there would be my HiFi system. I love to listen to music but my room would have to be soundproofed so as not to disturb my Mum and Dad.

b) My treasured HiFi would occupy the best position in the room. Naturally my ideal room would have to be soundproofed so that I could turn up the volume and my tone-deaf parents could still watch EastEnders in peace!

They use the same subject matter yet b) is livelier, uses more adjectives and through the use of the exclamation mark shows a stronger sense of audience.

Once you have completed your writing task use the time you have left to check, correct and, wherever possible, improve your work.

Helpful hints and reminders

Arrive for your examination in good time and well prepared. Make sure you have checked which paper you are taking and reminded yourself of what you will be required to do. Remember, for Paper 2 you need to take your **Anthology** with you.

Reading the paper

Read the questions and any written materials carefully. Take your time. It is essential that you do not rush at this very important stage.

Make sure you understand what you are being asked to do. Read the instructions and each question carefully. Where you have a choice of questions it is important that you choose the one you are best able to answer.

It may help you to underline or highlight important words or phrases in the instructions or questions or in the reading materials where appropriate. If you do make notes these should be single words or phrases. Do not waste time copying out chunks from the material.

Wherever appropriate, identify task, purpose and audience.

Planning your ideas

It's worrying how many people don't give sufficient time to this part of the process and simply start writing. Thinking time is essential and if you don't stop to think and plan your ideas before writing your whole piece of work will be badly affected.

Depending on the task you need to decide:

- *what* you are going to say
- the *order* in which you are going to say it
- *how* you are going to say it.

Remember, the plan is for your benefit and use only, so it has to mean something to you.

Presentational features

Think about additional presentational features you may need to include. Here are some things to consider:

- the layout of a letter, leaflet or news article
- appropriate use of headings and sub-headings
- underlining or block capitals for emphasis.

Writing effectively

While writing you should be thinking about how you can make most impact on your reader. Here are some things
to consider:

- expressing your ideas clearly

- referring to texts or materials where appropriate

- varying sentence structures and length

- using varied and interesting vocabulary that is appropriate to your audience.

Technical accuracy

As you are writing you should be constantly aware of:

- the need to paragraph appropriately

- the need to write clearly and legibly –
  if your examiner can't read your handwriting you're not likely to get many marks

- the need for accurate punctuation:
  full stops, commas, question marks, apostrophes, exclamation marks, speech and quotation marks are the main ones to remember

- the need for accurate spelling – make a determined effort to focus on the words you know you frequently get wrong;
  it is the silly mistakes that are always the most noticeable

- the need for clear expression of ideas – think each sentence through *before* you write it.

Keeping an eye on the time

There is no use writing brilliantly about one poem if you have been asked to write about two. Also, the examiner won't be impressed if you leave a story unfinished. Try to be constantly aware of the time you have in which to answer each question so that you can ensure your response is complete.

Checking your work

Leave five minutes at the end to check your work carefully. Read each word you have written – not what you think you have written. There is often a difference. Check that punctuation is clear and appropriate, e.g. have you put question marks at the end of your questions? Look for spelling or word mistakes you know you often make, e.g. 'of' instead of 'have', 'were' instead of 'we're', 'cant' instead of 'can't', 'there' instead of 'they're'. Above all, make sure that what you have written will make clear sense to the reader.